Getting Up

A True Path to Restoration & Fulfilling Your Destiny

J. Ashley Jensen

Copyright ©2011 J. Ashley Jensen
All rights reserved.
ISBN: 0615502156
ISBN 13: 9780615502151

Endorsements for Getting Up

"Ashley Jensen has written an uplifting account of the power of restoration. No matter how far one may feel from God, there is always a path back to grace and the great things destined for them. *Getting Up* will equip the reader with a biblical plan to overcome the things holding them back from a life of hope and fulfillment."

Matthew Barnett
Pastor & Co-founder, Los Angeles Dream Center
Best-selling author of The Cause Within You

"*Getting Up* has revelation and insight from a man who was not only knocked down, but had learned to stay down internally while showcasing a facade "having it all together." Ashley's brutal transparency is so refreshing. This book will help empower you to break the cycle of degradation, rise up, and become the champion God created you to be. If you're ready for real freedom read this book, walk it out, do it daily, and revel in the joy of not only Getting Up but Staying Up!"

Danny Chambers
Lead Pastor, Oasis Church

"This book serves as a rallying cry for those who have suffered elements of defeat in their lives. It simply makes the case that it is indeed possible to hold on to hope and see restoration."

Aaron Maners
Executive Pastor, Calvary Orlando

"We call them the 4 gospels because there's more than one way to share the Good News! Ashley's book, *Getting Up* has that freshness about it; a dynamic testimony and perspective on the gospel of Restoration!"

Gregg Johnson
International Speaker and Founder, J12

"Refreshing and rare... Enter the operating room of Ashley's heart surgery. You'll experience the inner life of a broken man. Ashley now healed extends an olive branch to us. Each page leaves you thinking, 'Maybe I can, maybe my brother can, maybe my husband can, maybe my son can be healed too.'"

Marcus Mecum
Lead Pastor, 7 Hills Church

"The great news about God's love is that He is always there to restore us if we truly want it. If you read this book and allow the principles to work it will change your life!"

Dennis & Colleen Rouse
Senior Pastors, Victory World Church

Table of Contents

Introduction..*Page ix*

Chapter 1   Sin Exposed..*Page 1*

Chapter 2   Personal Responsibility..................................*Page 25*

Chapter 3   Brokenness & Repentance............................*Page 43*

Chapter 4   Developing Self-Control & Accountability........*Page 65*

Chapter 5   Recovery & Restoration.................................*Page 87*

Chapter 6   Reaching Your Destiny ....*Page 105*

introduction

Take a brief moment and visit getupbook.com to view the chapter video introduction. These videos are a great resource to help deepen your understanding of the path to restoration.

A Captive in the Kingdom of Freedom

I leaned forward out of the dentist's chair, my mouth still numb, and mumbled a half-hearted thanks to my dentist for helping me out with a bad tooth. I was almost out the door when the dental assistant unexpectedly handed me a prescription. When I picked up my prescription for 40 pain pills, a shot of adrenaline surged through my veins, followed immediately by an uneasy feeling in the pit of my stomach. The little pill bottle in my hand was a reminder of the past I had left years ago – a past filled with living amidst a drug culture, dealing and doing drugs.

I felt as if I was doing something wrong, almost like I had just done a drug deal. Technically, I guess I had. Memories of parties, concerts, and people I had hung out with to get high started to overtake my mind. The thoughts were very uncomfortable, but very familiar. Then, just as suddenly, I snapped out of it. I said to myself arrogantly, "C'mon Ash, that was years ago, you're a pastor now, this stuff doesn't have a hold on you. Besides it's legal. It's just pain meds for some dental work." And so it began again. I had barely swallowed that first pain pill before I knew I was addicted again. That is when things started to drastically unravel on the inside of me.

At this time in my life, I had been given the opportunity as a youth pastor in my first full-time ministry position. I was seeing good success, in terms of what people think "success" looks like from the outside. The ministry was growing numerically, parents were on my side, and my pastor trusted me, even making sure I received a significant raise after my first year of being on staff. My wife was fooled; she thought I was doing just fine. She believed I was a man of integrity, hearing the voice of God, and leading our family the way she had always dreamed. I even fooled myself, justifying my behavior. I had failed morally and did not even recognize it.

It is sad to say but for the **season** of my life, I lived as a functional addict and alcoholic while in the ministry as a pastor. Drugs **and** alcohol had become an addictive escape. I lived as a captive inside the kingdom of freedom.

I moved on to another church position. Once again I had great success, but the sins of the flesh continued to plague me: lust, addiction, selfishness. I wallowed in it. Then a few injustices happened that impacted our family and rocked my faith in church leadership. Suddenly I had a reason to continue in sin. Unforgiveness and bitterness became bedrock. I had someone to blame other than myself. Now it was their fault that I was drinking and using drugs! My behavior was justified.

It reminds me of a time when I was doing yard work. As I began edging the patio, I moved a fairly large rock that hadn't been moved in a while and I noticed a whole little prehistoric world under there. Slimy, gross creatures that hadn't seen the light of day in ages started crawling for their lives! This was the perfect picture of my heart. Unforgiveness and bitterness had been allowed to live there so long they had grown into slimy, gross things that I kept hidden from the light of God. Disgusting things grow in the dark and we must beware of them.

My thinking and actions did not line up with my belief system. I knew I had to change, but complacency had set in. I just did not care anymore. Little by little my wife started to discover the things I had hidden. Before long I found myself on the verge of divorce, fired from a couple ministry positions at two really great churches, with two drug rehabs and one sexual rehab under my belt and enough NA (Narcotics Anonymous) white tags to tile a bathroom floor! (White tags represent your initial decision to give up narcotics.) By all means I was finished with the life I once wanted and my dreams of serving God on a public level were over. Destiny had passed me by and there was no good reason why I would ever be back in ministry. I continued to relapse and chose to wallow in continual sin until I finally hit rock bottom.

Everyone has a bottom. Once you hit the bottom though, there is good news. There is nowhere to go but up! I pray you find your "rock bottom" before the results of your decisions kill every relationship and opportunity you have available. I pray you will make the changes that will help you get on the path to true restoration. If you have found your bottom, then it is time to get up.

I have been around successful leaders long enough to know that people who do significant things for God and who make an eternal impact on the world around them usually have an epiphany of some sort. They typically have some divine encounter or life experience that shapes them as a person and sets them on a completely different trajectory in life. For me it came in a very unique way.

Rock bottom led me to my second rehab. Two weeks in, I discovered this was a different kind of treatment center. It was not one of those cushy palaces with landscaped lawns and pristine fountains. This place was in the middle of a field in the middle of nowhere. Not only did we learn how to overcome addiction, but we also went to church. We went to church a lot. It was what I called "Jesus-hab." To be honest, I went to this place never really intending to quit using drugs or alcohol. I had been going through the motions for so long that this was just one more dance I would have to memorize. But something happened to me.

God happened.

I will remember it as long as I live. Every Wednesday night all the guys in Jesus-hab would ride together in a van we affectionately referred to as "The Druggy Buggy." We headed out to this dinky Baptist church way out in the country, ate dinner with very sweet seniors, and listened to a very senior minister preach to us for an hour. Coming from the modern church environments I had experienced in the past, I hated every minute of it. I was used to lights, fog machines, loud rocking guitars and drums, and this was so – not that.

I grew up southern Baptist. I remember staring at lots of pews with built-in finger holes. I would pretend I was about to get on a roller coaster and go for a ride - but unfortunately I would ride right into a nap on my dad's lap every Sunday. That's right...the most boring roller coaster on earth. Lots of Baptist hymnals and of course hardback New King James Bibles for those unspiritual people who didn't bring their Bibles to church. That was me! Then there are the mini-golf pencils I'd use to write notes and draw pictures. Ah yes, the memories!

This Wednesday night was particularly unusual. After we had eaten and all the guys were outside smoking cigarettes, I decided to break away and be by myself. I was sitting in this little tiny Baptist church all alone waiting for service to start, looking at all the hymnals, the Bibles, the pews, the mini-golf pencils...things started to get really nostalgic. Then, I looked up at the stained glass window. While I was staring at a picture of Jesus, I started to remember the vision God had given me when I first got saved - a moment that will be etched into my memory forever. The vision of reaching countless numbers of people for Christ. The vision of writing books, speaking all over the world, and leading leaders. The vision of building the church through the gifts God had placed in me. Then, I started to think about about the two beautiful little girls God had entrusted to me, expecting me to be their father. I thought about the calling that God had laid on me when I was 20 years old. I had only just begun to scratch the surface of that calling. I thought about what could be and what should be.

Without warning the Holy Spirit exploded in my heart. The next thing I knew, I was on the floor in tears, weeping before God, repenting, and crying out, asking that He would forgive me, change me, and use me again. I decided to move forward, to move to the next level of living, to move into the destiny that still awaited me. I started to implement the steps laid out in this book and my life has never been the same.

So what was the deal? I started off really in love with God and wanting to serve Him and help people. How did I get so far off track? How did I end up almost ruining my life?

Maybe you have asked these same questions.

Maybe not.

Maybe you are just sick of feeling guilty. Maybe you just are tired of being ruled by sin and you think you have tried everything to break free from its hold. Maybe you just want to live the life God intended for you, but you cannot seem to get from point A to point B.

Maybe like me you have screwed up so badly that you think it is useless and you will never live your God-given destiny.

I may not know you or your situation, but one thing I do know is that I have lived in two places before. Not geographically, but spiritually. I have lived in bondage, and I have lived in freedom. Let me tell you, freedom is a lot better. I am living there right now and my prayer is you will too. The process laid out in this book is how I got up and got here, to this place called "freedom." Your journey will look very different from mine, but I am certain that the principles and practical steps in this book will help you. They may help you gain understanding as to why you do the things you do. They may help you understand the excuses and weak justifications of your actions. They may help you understand the significance of your role in the lives of those around you.

Whatever your story is, I believe these insights will help you, like they have me and countless others. They will help you learn how to be restored and live in a place called, "Freedom."

● ● ●

The First Step

I would be amiss if I didn't mention this first step. God has a purpose and plan for everyone. He loves everyone. Specifically, He loves you. This book is written for the Christian, by a Christian. My goal is not to bully or shame you into becoming a Christian. Plenty of people have done a great job of that through the ages with little or nothing to show for it. My goal is to help you discover life. Real life.

The process of restoration is a hard one, but if you could see what's on the other side you would throw your arms wide open and do whatever it takes to get there. Establishing a relationship with God is the first step. Please, do me favor, even though you probably do not even know me: give God a shot. Give as much effort to this God-thing as humanly possible. Everyone I have seen who has genuinely done this has never been the same.

Starting off right means starting (or getting back to) a relationship with God through His son Jesus Christ. You may have said "the sinner's prayer" a billion times. You may have attended a few (or a few hundred) church services. Maybe you have reached a "new state of consciousness," talked with a "spiritual advisor," or grew up in church as a preacher's kid. None of those things have any validation with God or automatically make you a Christian – or even halfway spiritual. Please understand having a relationship with and faith in Jesus Christ is the only way to achieve salvation and real communion with God.

Applying the principles found within this book – or in the Bible for that matter – will help you in the short-term, but for lasting change and eternal transformation you can never cancel out a thriving relationship with the living God. Just receiving His principles and not Him results in a humanized, secular gospel that has the outward appearance of godliness but in its nature denies the power of Holy Spirit. This will become a life that looks like the one the Apostle Paul describes in 2 Timothy 3:1-9, one that eventually leads to folly and foolishness.If you are at a place where there is absolute uncertainty about your relational standing with God, stop reading this book, pick up a Bible, and go to Romans 10:8-11. Simply go to Him in prayer and ask Him to come into your life. Confess Jesus as your Lord, but more than just saying it, believe it. God doesn't care how you pray; He just wants to hear you speak to Him.

Please understand, this is just barely scratching the surface on prayer and what it means to have a relationship with God. There are many resources available to you to learn more about growing as a Christian, and I encourage you to discover and devour as much as you can, starting with the Bible. For now though, you need to establish a new or renewed connection to the life-giving power of God that will help you through the process of restoration.

My prayer is that you read and apply this book, implement daily habits of spiritual growth, and get plugged into a life-giving, Bible-based church. I believe this will help the restorative process. From there, my hope is that your relationship with God is more amazing than you could have ever imagined!

Chapter 1
Sin Exposed

Take a brief moment and visit etupbook.com to view Chapter Video 1. This video describes the beginning of the restoration process.

Crazy Awakening

> 1 John 1:6-7 NIV
>
> *If we claim to have fellowship with him yet walk in the darkness, we lie and do not live by the truth. But if we walk in the light, as he is in the light, we have fellowship with one another, and the blood of Jesus, his Son, purifies us from all sin.*

I woke up one morning after a week of binge drinking and doing various narcotics, looked around, and did not recognize where I was. Well, physically I knew right where I was - in my second rehab. Spiritually, I was fumbling around in the dark. I did remember I had a choice to make: I could either continue to live a secret life of addiction or take the path of restoration. Choosing the path of restoration brought with it the painful memories of my actions: remembering that I had lost my job at a successful mega-church because of drug use… remembering that my wife and I were on the verge of a painful divorce because of years of lies…remembering that I was flat broke without two nickels to rub together!

I am in a room with four other guys in a treatment center in the middle of Nowheresville, Georgia. I'm talking, way out in the country. Like, you could shoot-a-cannonball-and-not-hit-anything country! The sobering reality is setting in.

Life as I knew it is now over.

I am in a place I do not want to be and surrounded by people I do not want to be around. People who have "real problems." Although it was a pretty hazy time of my life, I remember thinking to myself, "My bunkmate is a drug dealing oxycontin addict, this other guy is a life-long alcoholic, and the last guy in this room is a crystal meth cook! These dudes belong in rehab, but not me! I mean, I smoked a little pot, had some drinks, and popped some Valium. What's the big deal? I was just trying to relax! I don't belong here, this is crazy!" I actually thought I had some valid points.

God did not think so. To Him, my points were just as crazy as my behavior. My wife did not think so; she saw only a weak shell of the godly young man she had married. My pastors did not think so; they saw a creative, talented guy with a ton of potential choosing to waste his life.

Was it crazy that I was stuck in rehab – again? No. What is crazy is how I thought I could live the double-life I was living and still have some standing with God, fulfilling the call He had on my life. What is crazy is how I thought I could lie to my wife, my children, my pastors, and everyone around me about the sin I was holding on to and still think that I would have their respect. What is crazy is how I thought those other guys around me had real problems and I did not.

That is crazy.

The crazier thing is that I should have started this process years earlier! As restoration began its work in me, I realized I am the perfect candidate for God's healing power. So are you. As a matter of fact, everyone is.

I am not going to go into a bunch of details about my childhood, giving you the typical story of a spotty past. I am not going to describe in detail the life of sin I have lived. I am not writing this book to drudge up the past or blame anyone for my personal choices. I will say that just like everybody else, my childhood, my teenage years - pretty much my whole life - has not been perfect, not by a long stretch. Searching our past and pinpointing where things went wrong is extremely important and helpful, but that's not what this book is about. I wrote this book so that we could start off with today. How do we stand in the right-here-and-now and move forward with our lives?

My hope is that this book, some of my story, and the story of King David and some other folks in the Bible will help you gain insight and find answers to this daunting question. You can have the life you were created for and meant to live. I hope this book helps you believe that again.

● ● ●

Painful but Necessary

At some point, in some way, sin does get exposed. We can manage it and try to hide it, but it will get exposed. Unfortunately, pride and arrogance seem to ruin the chances of repentance, because we go into self-preservation mode - we talk about this in the next chapter. Sin is always exposed, either in public or in private. No matter where it comes out, we must realize it is always lain bare in the eyes of God.

HEBREWS 4:13 NLT

Nothing in all creation is hidden from God. Everything is naked and exposed before his eyes, and he is the one to whom we are accountable.

If we say we are a Christian and we want to be led by the Holy Spirit, there is no way we can live a life of continual sin and at the same time live a life completely dedicated to God. The equation just will not add up. God has such an immense love for us that there is no way He can allow us to continue in sin if we want to live the life he intended for us. That's right, it is His love for us that allows the sin to be exposed. What we usually have a problem with is the results of our sin being exposed. Those are called the consequences of sin. Sin being exposed is an act of love that God allows in our lives. The consequences of those things that were hidden are all on us.

Sin can be exposed in a number of different ways. You can get caught in the act of it, someone else can confront you on it, or the guilt and shame can be so heavy that you just have to tell someone about it. No matter how it happens, sin must be brought into the light and when it is… it is usually dragged kicking and screaming the whole way! Regardless of the situation, it will and must be exposed in order for you to get up and move forward.

The pain of sin being exposed is the worst thing I can imagine. I have broken my ankle and had it surgically screwed back together. I have fractured both wrists and had countless sprains from years of skateboarding and other sports. I have been jumped and beat up by three or more guys on a couple different occasions, and I got the snot kicked out of me back in my teenage years. I have been in multiple car accidents resulting in a broken sternum, a few broken ribs, a punctured lung, and a broken nose. Talk about pain; yeah, I have had my share for sure, and probably so have you!

The thing is, I can easily say those physically painful experiences do not even compare with the extreme pain of having the ugliness of my sin laid bare in the light of God and those around me. The pain seems unbearable. It is like being skinned alive, having every sick secret exposed for all to see. That is why we hide our sin, because we know when it comes out (and I did say 'when' not 'if') it is really going to hurt. Really, really hurt. I can tell you this, though: no matter how painful the truth may feel, the life of secret sin is way more painful. It hardens our hearts and rots our spirit. The old saying, "You're only as sick as your secrets" actually rings true, according to God's word.

> Psalm 32:2-4 NLT
> *Yes, what joy for those*
> *whose record the Lord has cleared of guilt,*
> *whose lives are lived in complete honesty!*
> *When I refused to confess my sin,*
> *my body wasted away,*
> *and I groaned all day long.*
> *Day and night your hand of discipline*
> *was heavy on me.*
> *My strength evaporated like water*
> *in the summer heat.*

The psalmist who wrote these words, David, knew the weight that sin carried. It obviously affected him even down to the very core of who he was! No matter how painful, sin must be exposed, somehow, in some way, in order for true healing and restoration to take place.

● ● ●

Wounds Require Healing and Healing Produces Scars

> *"Scar tissue is stronger than regular tissue. Realize the strength, move on."*
>
> -Henry Rollins, Henry Rollins Band

This quote is great for motivation! We have probably all heard quotes like this or similar thoughts. Another one says, "Whatever doesn't kill us makes us stronger." Although these make for awesome one-liners to help us push through some of the more painful seasons of life, they are not entirely true. My belief is that God wants us whole and healed completely, through every fiber of our being, not to just push through the pain of one more day to make it to the next.

Opposite to popular belief, scar tissue is not as strong as regular tissue. Henry Rollins was a great punk rocker, but he is not a doctor. I researched the real truth about scars and here is what I found.

> *"When sutures are removed, usually at the end of the first week, wound strength is approximately 10% of the strength of unwounded skin, but it increases rapidly over the next 4 weeks. This rate of increase then slows at approximately the third month after the original incision and then reaches a plateau at about 70 to 80% of the tensile strength of unwounded skin, which may persist for life."*
>
> -Robbins Pathologic Basis of Disease

So there you have it! It is never 100% healed. It could get that way, eventually, but for the most part it is 70-80% of what it was originally. We would think by looking at a scar that it would be stronger because usually it is numb, tough, and inflexible. So it must mean scars are stronger. Not really. It is just not medically true. It is a scar for a reason. An injury occurred and that is the spot where a healing has taken place. I can bet that if that scar were re-injured again and again, it would hurt twice as much as the first time and hurt even more the next time. Not to mention that it would take even longer to heal properly, because it's a weak spot. The only thing that is stronger is the tissue surrounding it.

It is interesting to note that God calls us "the body of Christ." A healthy physical body heals itself. The skin around that scar is its strength. The people in your life, the people in the body of Christ around you should be a strong part of your healing and restoration. They can never help you if your sin remains in the dark. It must come out in order to truly live the way God intended.

When sin takes place in a person's life it's actually a choice of death.

> Romans 6:23 NKJV
>
> *For the wages of sin is death, but the gift of God is eternal life in Christ Jesus our Lord.*

We like to focus on the last part of that verse because of the promise of salvation, but our focus does not make the first part of that verse any less true. Death will happen because of sin: the death of a marriage, death of an opportunity, death of a dream and maybe even death of our earthly destiny if the sin is continued in long enough. Sin is like a continual injury to healed scar tissue. It cuts like a knife and healing must take place. What appears is the scar over and over.

We think because we have tasted some healing in that area of our life and we have some scar tissue to show that we are numb to it. We feel we are tough in that area now and we can move on. We think it means we will not be compromised. We have an inflexible war wound to show off. We can handle it now.

Absolutely wrong.

We must realize our scars are weak spots. They are NOT tougher. They can be re-injured at any moment if we are not protective of the area of our lives where God is bringing freedom and healing. One day we will be strong - even strong enough to help others - but in the process of restoration we cannot be naïve. We do not know it all and we do not have all the answers. We must allow the healing process to take place. When we think about the life of sin we lived, at the core of who we are, there is unrest. There is an un-peaceful feeling in our hearts, if not a lump in our throats, because we see the ugliness of the scar. We see our weak spot for what it is. The beautiful thing about God, though, is that He will resurrect dead things if we operate in faith and obedience to Him.

How Did This Happen?

Let's think about this for a second. We are saved by the amazing blood of Jesus Christ, filled with the awe-inspiring power of the Holy Spirit, and most likely plugged into a beautiful community of believers called the church. Or at least, we could be, with a church on virtually every corner! God also gives us gifts to use for His glory and sometimes His grace allows those gifts to be used to make a living. Not to mention, if you live in America, you are in the top 6% of the wealthiest people in the world! So how does this happen? How is it we can look around, seem to have everything, and then make a conscious decision to sin?

People have struggled with this question for a very long time. I will try and scratch the surface from my own experience. For me, it was a similar to a mathematic equation.

$$PRIDE + SELFISHNESS + BITTERNESS \times JUSTIFICATION = CONTINUAL\ SIN$$

This deadly, ninja-quick combination of character assassins will tap out even the boldest of Christians, if not uprooted quickly. For you, your formula for progressive and continual sin may look very different. Regardless of what the formula is, it must be recognized, confronted, and brought into the light.

• • •

Learning from a King

I love the story of David. His story is the American dream. It's like a 'Rocky' movie, a true underdog story if we have ever heard one! He starts out in life as an unknown shepherd boy, the runt of the family, pretty much nobody of any importance. I challenge you to read his story. It truly is amazing. Our focus in this chapter, though, is not his whole story. Instead I want to focus on one tiny, dark slice in the life of David that had huge implications. I believe we will be shocked at how similar our life might look in comparison to David's.

2 SAMUEL 11:1-4 NLT

In the spring of the year, when kings normally go out to war, David sent Joab and the Israelite army to fight the Ammonites. They destroyed the Ammonite army and laid siege to the city of Rabbah. However, David stayed behind in Jerusalem. Late one afternoon, after his midday rest, David got out of bed and was walking on the roof of the palace. As he looked out over the city, he noticed a woman of unusual beauty taking a bath. He sent someone to find out who she was, and he was told, "She is Bathsheba, the daughter of Eliam and the wife of Uriah the Hittite." Then David sent messengers to get her; and when she came to the palace, he slept with her.

This whole story is jacked up. It starts out jacked up, it continues jacked up, and it ends jacked up. We are just at the beginning, but within these 4 small verses, these tiny lines of black letters on white paper, we can see the beginning of monumental and life-changing events for David.

Let's look at some things that contributed to David's slippery slope of sin. My hope is that it helps us examine our own lives also.

Spiritual Laziness

King David was one of the greatest leaders to ever live! Military strategists study the strategies of David and even employ them to this very day. David was a timeless leader, but no matter how great of a leader you are, you must always be on your game. The scripture indicates it was spring, when kings go off to war. This was an important time for kings in that day, the time when they defended their territory or took new ground. This was the time when the leaders go and lead!

But David did not. He decided to sit this one out. Instead, David sent his right hand man, Joab, to go lead the team and fight the battle. This was David's first step toward sin. Maybe I am reading into the scripture a bit, but I am willing to bet this wasn't the first time David had done this. It seems it is just the first time we get to read about it.

David was a war hero. By this point he had fought and won many battles. His body was probably tattered, beat up, and scarred from the training and hand-to-hand combat he had experienced. It is safe to say he probably did not even get too involved in the actual firefight of war at this point in his life. Perhaps he believed that his only value was in creating strategies and helping others lead thousands of men to victory.

> **We can never abdicate to someone else the thing that only we can do.**

We can never abdicate to someone else the thing that only we can do. David was such a great leader, someone who had raised up so many other great leaders, and he *knew* that Joab and the army would crush the enemy. The scripture goes on to say that is exactly what happened. The problem was, David *knew it*. He allowed his arrogance to blind him to his responsibilities.

There's a difference between God-confidence and self-confidence. When God is the catalyst for great things that happen around us, it feels so good, even natural. It feels so natural that we can cross the line and slip into taking credit for the success we have experienced rather than deflecting it back to the Lord. I believe this is what happened to David.

The other thing we need to take note of is that David was just waking up from a nap. The scripture says, "after his midday rest." A nap? He was supposed to be off at war, but instead he was taking a nap! "What's wrong with a nap?" you may ask. Nothing. I love naps. I believe naps are glorious things –creations of the Lord God himself.

What I think is so interesting is that the Bible specifically says that he was taking a nap. It seems to indicate that David was kind of being extra lazy. It could have left that whole "nap" part right out of the story and it still would have made perfect sense. Yet, the nap was mentioned as if it were a daily occurrence. That phrase seems to have been included on purpose, almost as if to tell us something. I believe it is telling us that we cannot afford to get spiritually lazy. Sounds like David was getting soft. It seems he was skipping out on the responsibilities of leading and instead was enjoying "the good life"... just chillin' out.

The first step on the slippery slope of sin is now revealed. Spiritual laziness sets in. David allowed the comfort of his life bring him to a place of complacency. Complacency and apathy are always the first step towards sin. The thing about spiritual laziness is you don't notice it at first. Complacency is a creeper. It starts with a thought. Maybe you miss your quiet time. No big deal, you think, you will catch up with it tomorrow. But tomorrow comes and goes, and your quiet time came and went with it! Maybe you used to be at church every time the doors were open, but now it is just a faded memory of the good ole' days.

The Komodo Dragon of Complacency

Complacency reminds me of this crazy show I have seen about people who keep wild animals as pets. In one particular episode, a guy had some exotic lizards and monitors as pets. These animals roamed freely in his apartment! He would hand feed these animals and talk to them as if they were family. It turns out he was bitten by one of these massive beasts while he was feeding them. He was under the assumption he would be fine because he had built up immunity to the venom, so he did not seek medical attention. Over the course of the next few days he became violently ill, not realizing it was the venom working its way through his body.

It is important to note here, the animal that bit him was a Komodo dragon. Within the dragon's venom is a compound that decreases blood pressure, eventually sending the prey into shock, causing it to collapse and eventually die. The Komodo can then dine at leisure. Here is the part that reminds me of complacency: the venom takes days, maybe even up to a week, to work through the prey's body before it collapses. All the while, the Komodo dragon is tracking and stalking, waiting for its victim to be too weak to defend itself against the predator.

> Complacency is venom that shoots right to the heart of who we are.

Unfortunately, it was a physically gruesome outcome for the man involved in this story. All too often, there is a pretty gruesome outcome for the spiritually lazy. Complacency is venom that shoots right to the heart of who we are. We become comfortable in our surroundings, our family, our career, and scariest of all, our relationship with God. Before we know it, the fire has gone out and we leave ourselves open to attacks we are too weak to defend against.

Living Inside Out

The exterior will eventually become a reflection of our interior. We can put on a good act and hide out for a while, but eventually what is on the inside will surface on the outside. Jesus said in Luke 6:45, "For out of the abundance of the heart, his mouth speaks."

> The exterior will eventually become a reflection of our interior

What is in our heart will eventually come out, in our words and our actions. Jesus even got right to the heart of the fakers and haters of his day – the scribes and the Pharisees.

> MATTHEW 23:25-28 NKJV
>
> *Woe to you, scribes and Pharisees, hypocrites! For you cleanse the outside of the cup and dish, but inside they are full of extortion and self-indulgence. Blind Pharisee, first cleanse the inside of the cup and dish, that the outside of them may be clean also.*

> *Woe to you, scribes and Pharisees, hypocrites! For you are like whitewashed tombs which indeed appear beautiful outwardly, but inside are full of dead men's bones and all uncleanness. Even so you also outwardly appear righteous to men, but inside you are full of hypocrisy and lawlessness.*

It is safe to say that Jesus could not stomach the double life people try to live on his behalf. We must be on guard at all times when it comes to keeping our spiritual passion alive and well. Feeding the fire of God involves times of conversation and prayer with the Lord, soaking in God's presence through personal times of worship, reading and studying the scripture, having conversations with your spouse or a close friend about what God is doing in your life, and talking to people relationally about the goodness of God.

If we can catch complacency before it even happens, we could prevent the one act of sin that can ruin years of our life. If we do not catch it, we can find ourselves steadily sliding down towards the next step.

Spiritual Amnesia - Don't Believe The Hype!

The other thing that happens is what I like to call "Spiritual Amnesia." Typically, amnesia is caused by an injury, some sort of head trauma. Spiritual amnesia is exactly the opposite. It usually starts to set in when things are going really well, really comfy. Life is great, the bills are paid, and not only are we living the American dream…we ARE the American dream. People start to compliment us, looking to us to fix their problems, and eventually we become a functional savior for people. We eventually start to believe our own hype.

No one was built for that. Jesus was and is the only One who can handle that type of pressure.

That's exactly what happened to David. He believed his own hype. He got all bowed up in his mind. He got comfortable and began to forget. He not only forgot who he was, he forgot what God had done for him. He forgot it was God who delivered him from the lion and the bear as a shepherd boy. He forgot it was God who supernaturally sunk the stone in Goliath's head. He forgot it was God who paved the way so he could become the king of Israel.

At this point, I think it is imperative we slow our roll on judging David and find a bit of balance and perspective. We have all been this way. We all forget who we are without God. We forget that he has blessed each us infinitely more than we deserve. Maybe more importantly, we forget who we are in Christ.

Herein lies the interesting thing about spiritual amnesia. It is not that we forgot – it is that we cannot remember. There is a block of some sort that just will not allow us to remember the amazing things God has done for us. We get so blinded by our appetites that our spiritual memory bank gets all clogged up and we can only think of one thing – what can satisfy my desire right now? Selfishness clouds our memory.

It is amazing to see the link between forgetfulness and pride. I am not sure of the exact succession of these steps. I have experienced both in my life - pride then forgetfulness, forgetfulness then pride. In either case the result is devastating to our destiny. Moses even called it out early in the Old Testament, warning an entire nation about the dangers of forgetfulness, which will lead to pride.

Deuteronomy 8:10-20 NASB (my emphasis added in bold)

*"When you have eaten and are satisfied, you shall bless the Lord your God for the good land which He has given you. Beware that you **do not forget the Lord your God** by not keeping His commandments and His ordinances and His statutes which I am commanding you today; otherwise, when you have eaten and are satisfied, and have built good houses and lived in them, and when your herds and your flocks multiply, and your silver and gold multiply, and all that you have multiplies, **then your heart will become proud and you will forget the Lord your God** who brought you out from the land of Egypt, out of the house of slavery. He led you through the great and terrible wilderness, with its fiery serpents and scorpions and thirsty ground where there was no water; He brought water for you out of the rock of flint. In the wilderness He fed you manna which your fathers did not know, that He might humble you and that He might test you, to do good for you in the end. Otherwise, **you may say in your heart, 'My power and the strength of my hand made me this wealth.'** But **you shall remember the Lord your God**, for it is He who is giving you power to make wealth, that He may confirm His covenant which He swore to your fathers, as it is this day. It shall come about if you ever **forget the Lord your God** and go after other gods and serve them and worship them, I testify against you today that you will surely perish. Like the nations that the Lord makes to perish before you, so you shall perish; because you would not listen to the voice of the Lord your God."*

The scripture makes it so plain how we can just flat out forget and let subtle spiritual amnesia creep in, which leads us to pride. For me, I keep in mind on a daily basis the blessings God has shown in my life. Some call it a "gratitude list," some say it is as simple as counting your blessings. I know that I start my day with thankfulness, taking an inventory of the greatness that surrounds me. I have breath in my lungs, I can walk and talk, and I have a roof over my head and food in my belly. From there, it is just icing on the cake! My beautiful wife, amazing kids, and a job! After that it just gets ridiculous how much God has blessed us!

There is so much we have to be thankful for. It is up to us to thank Him for it, lest we get diagnosed with a gnarly case of spiritual amnesia.

• • •

Sin Has Unusual Beauty

As we get back to the narrative of David, it says David saw Bathsheba and took notice of her 'unusual beauty.' I have always found that description a little interesting. Really? As if she was the only super hot chick in Israel? I highly doubt it. At this point David had seven wives and many concubines; the Bible is not clear on how many, but at least ten (2 Samuel 20:3). It was not like David was starved for affection. It was not that he just had to have sex. "Unusual beauty" tempted him in a moment of weakness, selfishness, and complacency.

The temptations that we take notice of will always have "unusual beauty." The enemy is stupid and smart at the same time. He is stupid because he tempts you in the same area over and over again, and he is smart because he tempts you in the same area over and over again.

Wait, what? You said the same thing.

Exactly. The enemy has a plan for you and your areas of weakness. Your weakness will always be your weakness. I believe you can be free from sin absolutely, but temptation will always present itself. Your weakness will not be the same as mine and my weakness will not be the same as yours, but one thing is guaranteed: we all have a weakness. When temptation presents itself, it will take on an 'unusual beauty' and attack us at our weakest point. We must recognize it for what it is… a sharp knife ready to slice open a healed scar.

The problem is, we do not recognize it. We give in to the temptation. Our sinful flesh tells our intellectual brain to come up with a good reason why we must have this unusually beautiful thing. This is when the justification starts to set in, which leads us to the next step in the process.

Taking the Leap

> *2 Samuel 11:2 NLT*
>
> *…was walking on the roof of the palace. As he looked out over the city…*

The palace seems to have been set higher than the entire city. David had a view of the whole place. But instead of enjoying the view of his kingdom, relishing in thankfulness for what God had done for him, he focused on the one "unusually beautiful" thing.

David was about to commit suicide. He was on top of the tallest building in the city about to jump off the edge, not literally but spiritually. He was about to bring spiritual death to part of his life.

It is interesting and almost comical when I hear the term "fall into sin." It is as if we are running along in the middle of broad daylight and out of nowhere, a huge hole appears and we just fall right into it. Another term I find kind of funny is "I struggle with this sin." No we don't. If we struggled with it there would be an indication of a fight.

I watch a lot of mixed martial arts, which involves a lot of wrestling and Brazilian ju jitsu. The thing I have noticed during this kind of grappling is that these guys are in a fight; they are in a struggle. When they go back to their corners they are tired, sweaty, and usually bloody. Their faces look all beat up, and sometimes they are limping or can barely move at all! They have been in a struggle, a real fight.

Let's ask a couple questions:

- Is that what we look like after we have sinned?
- Do we look like we've been in a struggle?

Usually not. Usually temptation comes knocking and we do not even put up a fight. It is as if we step in the ring, tap out immediately, and submit to sin before the fight bell even rings! I know this from my own experience - any time I actually put up a fight and resist temptation, it goes away.

> *JAMES 4:7 NKJV*
> *Therefore submit to God. Resist the devil and he will flee from you.*

The Bible is clear. It does not mince words. If we want freedom, we can have it, if we truly resist temptation. That is why Christianese terms like "struggle with sin" or "fall into sin" irritate me so much! Even though I have used them many times, they are just a feeble attempt to make my sin seem more palatable or politically correct. It is not palatable and it is not politically correct! It is disgusting and we must develop a hatred for it!

The bottom line is we do not fall into sin; we jump! We full on take the cannonball position and make a flying leap into the pool of sin. This is what David did. He jumped off the tallest building he could find when he sinned with Bathsheba.

Take the Gloves Off

It is time to take the gloves off and go bare knuckle brawling after the sin that has knocked us out for years. It is our time to get motivated and fired up to actually struggle with sin, because when we put up an actual fight, we win.

Chapter 2
Personal Responsibility

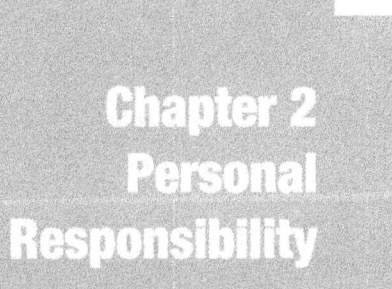

Take a brief moment and visit getupbook.com to view Chapter Video 2. This video talks about the importance of taking personal responsibility and how it affects the process of restoration.

Taking it on the Chin

> *1 JOHN 1:8 NIV*
>
> *If we claim to be without sin, we deceive ourselves and the truth is not in us.*
>
> *1 JOHN 1:10 NIV*
> *If we claim we have not sinned, we make him out to be a liar and his word has no place in our lives.*

Personal responsibility is something that we just cannot seem to do right off the bat. It seems we want to justify, blame-shift, or straight up deny the truth rather than just own up to it. In every facet of society, it is easy to see that personal responsibility is hard to come by. If we ever want to truly find restoration and real life, this area cannot be overlooked. We must take personal responsibility for our actions.

So why is it so hard to do? Well, it started way before you and I were here. Taking responsibility for our actions has been a battle in the heart of man since the Garden of Eden and continues to this very day.

The Garden Blame Game

> *GENESIS 3:7-8 NKJV*
>
> *Then the eyes of both of them were opened, and they knew that they were naked; and they sewed fig leaves*

together and made themselves coverings. And they heard the sound of the Lord God walking in the garden in the cool of the day, and Adam and his wife hid themselves from the presence of the Lord God among the trees of the garden.

Let's catch up on the back-story here. Satan, who was in the garden as the serpent, came and tempted Eve with eating the fruit from the tree of the knowledge of good and evil – the fruit God said not to eat. She jumped in and took a bite of the forbidden fruit. Eve then influenced Adam to do the same thing. So now both of them had done the very thing God specifically told them not to do! They were in sin and they knew it.

What is the natural progression? Covering our sin. Hiding it so no one will find out, of course. They sewed fig leaves together and hid in the bushes. Let's get this straight…you are going to try and hide from the Creator of all things in the bushes. Really? That's laughable.

But don't we do the same thing? Don't we try to hide things from God, as if He doesn't already know what we have done even before we did it! We learned in the last chapter that sin will be exposed no matter how hard or how long we try and hide it.

> GENESIS 3:9
>
> *Then the Lord God called to Adam and said to him, "Where are you?"*

God asks Adam an obvious question, "Where are you?" Do you think God did not know where Adam was? Of course He did. God knows exactly where we are. He asks for our benefit, not His. He wants to know where we are relationally with Him. Is there something making us hide? Is there something we are so ashamed of that the only thing we know to do is to foolishly try and cover ourselves?

We all know we should just own up right away, but we always want to start at the game of blame. I wonder if this one question haunted Adam for the rest of his life. So now we enter the original blame game, or what I call "The Garden Blame Game." This is where it all started. It is amazing to watch how this all plays out.

> GENESIS *3:10-13 NKJV*
>
> *So he said, "I heard Your voice in the garden, and I was afraid because I was naked; and I hid myself." And He said, "Who told you that you were naked? Have you eaten from the tree of which I commanded you that you should not eat?" Then the man said, "The woman whom You gave to be with me, she gave me of the tree, and I ate." And the Lord God said to the woman, "What is this you have done?"*
>
> *The woman said, "The serpent deceived me, and I ate."*

If we read this passage closely we can see Adam and Eve squirming, trying to wiggle their way out of the truth almost instantly. God asked where Adam was and Adam responds with, "I was afraid because I was naked." Do you see that? He changes the subject right off the bat! Adam was afraid because he ate the fruit God told him not to eat, not because he was naked. Verse 7 already told us that he had sewed fig leaves together to cover himself, so he was not naked. He was fully clothed and hiding in the bushes! So God, infinitely wise, asks a set up question and then gets right to the heart of the matter. "Who told you that you were naked? Have you eaten from the tree of which I commanded you that you should not eat?"

Adam doesn't answer correctly, though. He does not just say, "Yes God, I ate the fruit." Instead he puts on his lawyer fig leaves, pulls out his court tablets and blames his wife, the wife God gave him. It is almost like he was saying, "It is your fault for giving her to me. If she wasn't hanging around we wouldn't be in this predicament!" No bueno, Adam. No good indeed.

God knows where Adam is, but in His mercy He gives Adam a chance to repent and get things right...but Adam blows it.

So God moves on to Eve. Maybe, just maybe she will take responsibility for her actions. Unfortunately the blame game continues. God asks Eve what she has done. He does not ask her who deceived her, but Eve volunteers that information thinking that God will hold her blameless. It is funny because she, like Adam, prefaces her statement with blame. Instead of just saying, "I ate the fruit", she feels the need to explain why she ate the fruit and who influenced her to do it.

The problem is that we have this self-preservation mechanism that throws up walls around our personal life. When sin does get exposed in our life, we want to deny it, blame-shift it to someone else or flat out not care and just continue in our sin and rebellion regardless of who we hurt or how our life is going. This did not work in the garden and it will not work now. We must take personal responsibility for our actions.

The crazy thing is Adam never really comes clean. The Bible is not clear on whether he fully admits to God what he has done or if Adam fully commits to taking personal responsibility. It makes me wonder if maybe things would have turned out differently for all of humanity if Adam had just taken full responsibility for what he had done.

The Missing Ingredient

Whenever someone gets in a situation where they try to pass the blame, you can usually dig a little deeper and find that their character and integrity is lacking. This is the missing ingredient. Let's think how things would be if everybody had strong character. Just imagine what it would look like if everybody had integrity. Many times people think character and integrity is the same thing. In fact, they are closely related, but there is a difference.

Take a Good Look in the Mirror

Character is the make up of a person. The thing about character is you can have weak character or strong character; it is up to you. We have all met those people who just seem to have everything together. You know the type. They have a clean car and their laundry is all done. They show up to every appointment on time, if not early. They are the teacher's pet and the boss's favorite, if it is not the boss themselves!

Yeah, I couldn't stand that person either...until I started to become that person. I realized I needed that in my life in order to fulfill the call God had on my life. The reality is, nobody is ever born with strong character, completely disciplined, and totally responsible. Theologically speaking, we are born into sin. The only character trait common to all of us is selfishness. Having strong character is something that is developed and will always need to be worked on constantly.

There are times when I take a good look in the mirror and there are some areas of my body I would like to improve physically. I look at my stomach and say, "Wow, it sure would be nice to have a six pack." Maybe I check out my chest and arms and think, "It would be sweet if I could be ripped by summer." Meanwhile I know full well that I just ate like a hog at Thanksgiving and the Christmas cookies and peanut butter fudge have caught up to me! What would be crazy is to think I can eat whatever I want and not do any type of physical activity and think that I can still reach my fitness goals. There is just no way that is going to happen.

Likewise, we need to take a good look in the mirror and check out our character. If there is something that is happening in the reflection of our character that needs improvement, we need to take action to change it. For instance, if we are constantly late to appointments, then there needs to be something in us that says, "No matter what is happening I will not be late. I will set my alarm, I will plan ahead, and no matter what I will be on time!"

Developing strong character takes resolve. There has to be a determination that you will better yourself through the power of the Holy Spirit. Character development is a learned behavior. After you do a thing over and over again it will become almost second nature to you, whether it is a negative or a positive behavior. The best way I have found to develop strong character is by practicing integrity.

The Strength of Your Character

Integrity is often defined as "having a sound moral character." I have a simple definition of integrity that I remind myself of often: "Integrity is the strength of your character." If I do not have integrity then I will have weak character.

For example, when a carpenter is setting the trusses on a house and is ready to deck the roof with plywood, he has to make sure that all of the trusses are solid and intact. He is looking at the integrity of the wood in order to determine if it can handle the weight of the plywood. By the time a carpenter has decked an entire roof with plywood, the weight of the roof can be several tons. Those trusses holding the plywood must have integrity. They must be strong!

Life is like the plywood that goes on a roof. It can be heavy. The trusses that plywood sits on are our character. Life can put an immense amount of pressure on us. We must have integrity, real strength of character, in order to carry the load and withstand the stress.

Practicing integrity is key to having strong character. Here are two ways to start off or to reinvent practicing integrity that will help to develop strong character:

1. Do what you say you will do and live what you say you believe.
> Jesus said in Matthew 5:37 to let your 'Yes be yes and your no be no." He was emphasizing that our words should seal the deal. We have all said certain things and then not followed through, but the development of integrity is in the act of following through.
>
> In most sports, there is a follow through motion that takes place. Regardless of the sport – whether you swing a club, bat, or a racket, kick or throw a ball, swing or kick a heavy bag – the power of what you are doing is in the follow through. The follow through helps direct the object to where you want it to go.
>
> When you say you will do something and you do it, your life will go the direction you want it to go because your actions make it happen. Make sure you follow through with what you

say you will do and what you say you believe. There is power in the follow through.

2. Develop a daily, spiritual growth plan.

Discipline breeds integrity. I read a great book about discipline a long time ago, appropriately named, "The Celebration of Discipline" by Richard Foster. This book helped me understand the importance of spiritual disciplines and how to practically implement them in my life. I highly recommend it and believe it will help you in the area of self-discipline.

By waking up early, Bible reading, praying, reading leadership books, or reading books in your area of passion, you will start to develop strong character. Making and keeping a daily appointment with God will build a strong foundation in your character development because it will build self-discipline in your life.

These may seem so elementary, but I have found if we can just practice these simple things on a daily basis, we will find our character will get stronger and stronger. Our integrity will continue to be developed and we will begin to see the results of that integrity. One thing I have learned being a Christian and in ministry is that God is way more concerned with our character than our career or our calling. Charisma will get us in the position, but character will keep us there. He would rather us live a humble life filled with integrity and never becoming a "success" than for us to be "successful" and giving His bride another black eye because of our lack of integrity.

● ● ●

Response Ability

> *"Look at the word responsibility—response-ability—the ability to choose your response."*
>
> *- Stephen R. Covey*

Personal responsibility is the ability to respond in a mature way to our personal choices. When we take personal responsibility it means we take the weight of the consequence or benefit of our actions. There are million and one things that can happen to us. God is concerned about those things, but I think He is more concerned with what happens *through* us than what happens *to* us. He wants see how we respond. He is interested in our character development, which includes how we respond to temptation or how we respond to the situations that can cause offense. This is our ability to respond. This is personal responsibility.

I liken response-ability to any ability in which we can grow. The more we perfect our response, the greater our ability grows. I would say this is a major key to growth and maturity, and absolutely essential to the process of getting up.

● ● ●

Looking in the Rearview

I have been in counseling, around counseling, and even counseled for a number of years. I have been in treatment centers. I have been in deliverance classes. I have been in a number of situations where I have had to get really honest with someone about my problems, and the first question I have always heard is about my childhood.

We usually find there is a situation that caused pain, damage, or trauma in our lives. If we have not properly dealt with the pain of it, it will continue to have the ability to cause problems in our lives. As we dig around in our past, we can often find the point when the issues that were beneath the surface started to manifest themselves in our thought life and eventually in our behavior. This is highly beneficial and I highly recommend it doing it with a counselor, but it's not the solution to our problem. It is just a starting point that can give us understanding, but it will never give us the answer.

There's a great one-liner I heard years ago, "Look at life through the windshield, not the rear view mirror." It seems that when things go wrong in our lives we want to look in the rear view to see what the heck we just hit. This must happen. We have to take an honest look at where we went wrong. We need to look at what happened to us, what someone did to us, or what we did to someone else. We have to take an honest inventory to find the root of the bad fruit in our lives.

The problem that I have seen happen, though, is once the thing is discovered we do not do anything about it. We use it as a scapegoat to place blame for why we continue to sin. We point at it and say, "It is that ugly thing over there, yeah, that is the real culprit! Not me!" So we blame the past for our behavior. We end up staring in the rear view instead of forgiving someone or going to get forgiveness from someone. We try and drive our life looking in the rear view the whole time. Eventually we will have a horrific crash if we do not focus on what is going on in the windshield!

> *Philippians 3:13-14 NLT*
>
> *No, dear brothers and sisters, I have not achieved it, but I focus on this one thing: Forgetting the past and looking forward to what lies ahead, I press on to reach*

the end of the race and receive the heavenly prize for which God, through Christ Jesus, is calling us.

I love the fact that the apostle Paul mentioned there is one thing, even if it is the only thing he does; he forgets the past. He goes on to say we must look through the windshield! The past is totally there, but you cannot change it and you cannot blame it. As a matter of fact, you cannot do anything about it except forget it!

Understanding this is of key importance to getting up and moving on into God's call for your life. You cannot hang on to old hurts, habits, or hang ups only to justify your sin and still think that you can continue in the destiny to which God has called you. The only productive and fruitful way to go is to own the fact that we alone are the only ones at fault for our actions.

• • •

You Are The Man

Let's jump back to the story of David and Bathsheba. In a state of pure lust, David sends for Bathsheba in order to have sex with her, and he does. But, something that David never thought about happens. That is always the case when we willfully sin – something happens that we never expected. Bathsheba gets pregnant.

Oh, snap. Not good.

> What you cover, God will uncover. What you uncover, God will cover.

David finds out about it and has the opportunity to take personal responsibility for his actions, but what does he do instead? He covers it up. Of course he does! Why confess when you can cover? It goes back to the self-preservation instinct. I have learned that what we cover, God will uncover, but what we uncover, God will cover. Love covers a multitude of sin but we must be willing to confess it.

Think about this: it is amazing that no matter what we do to try and cover our sin, it eventually comes out. We can go to extravagant lengths to sew together our fig leaves but regardless of what we do, God always knows where we are and He loves us too much to allow us to stay there.

To cover up the pregnancy, David brings her husband Uriah home from war - who was by the way, off fighting for King David! David sets things up for Uriah to sleep with his own wife, Bathsheba, at his own house, and even gets him drunk! Nonetheless, Uriah refuses to sleep with his own wife, saying it wouldn't be right for him to get to have a night of pleasure his wife while the other guys are off at war risking their lives.

At this point, David makes a terrible choice that not only affects him, but the rest of his lineage as well. He sends Uriah back to war and instructs the other men who are fighting with him to pull back at the time when the battle is at its worst. The time when your boys are supposed to have your back, they disappear and leave you on the battlefield all alone. Not too many men could handle a situation like that, and neither could Uriah. It is a set-up, and he is killed in the heat of battle. David has just committed cold-blooded murder in the first degree. Naturally, his next move is to marry the wife of the man he just murdered.

So, let's review here for a second. David sleeps with Uriah's wife and gets her pregnant, then kills her husband to cover up his own sin, and then marries the dead guy's wife. Wow. There's an old saying, "Sin will take you farther than you want to go, keep you longer than you want to stay, and cost you more than you're willing to pay." Now that is the truth. David did some dirty deeds to get what he wanted and then cover up what he actually got.

It is rather easy to look at someone else's sin and make a judgment call. Comparatively though, I think as we read the whole chapter of 2 Samuel 11 and think about our own life, I believe we will be shocked at just how far sin can drag us into deception. When we take the humble route and examine our own life, we can find that we probably are not much different.

There always needs to be someone in our lives who will bring truth to us, someone who will confront us with the disgusting image of our sin. If you are willing to walk with God and want to fulfill your calling, He will always provide this person. For David, it was a prophet named Nathan.

> 2 SAMUEL *12:1-8 NLT*
>
> *So the Lord sent Nathan the prophet to tell David this story: "There were two men in a certain town. One was rich, and one was poor. The rich man owned a great many sheep and cattle. The poor man owned nothing but one little lamb he had bought. He raised that little lamb, and it grew up with his children. It ate from the man's own plate and drank from his cup. He cuddled it in his arms like a baby daughter. One day a guest arrived at the home of the rich man. But instead of killing an animal from his own flock or herd, he took*

the poor man's lamb and killed it and prepared it for his guest."

David was furious. "As surely as the Lord lives," he vowed, "any man who would do such a thing deserves to die! He must repay four lambs to the poor man for the one he stole and for having no pity."

Then Nathan said to David, "You are that man! The Lord, the God of Israel, says: I anointed you king of Israel and saved you from the power of Saul. I gave you your master's house and his wives and the kingdoms of Israel and Judah. And if that had not been enough, I would have given you much, much more."

Nathan calls out the King. He basically says, "You are the man, David; you are the man." Usually being "the man" has benefits, but in this case, it was not all it is cracked up to be. Nathan cleverly told the king a story to see how he would respond. He dangled the emotional bait out there for David, who took it hook, line, and sinker. After that, Nathan brought the heat! He laid the truth out there in broad daylight.

When the truth is brought forth and we are confronted, our response means everything. Our response to sin determines our level of repentance, which can determine our level of restoration!

> Our response to sin determines our level of repentance, which can determine our level of restoration!

If we respond humbly and acknowledge our sin, allowing the full weight of what we have done to impact our heart and mind, then it leads to repentance. True repentance. If we respond with defensiveness and pride, then chances are we probably won't truly repent and eventually end up deeper in the deception of sin, living a fruitless, fake Christian life at best.

Think about David's situation. He was the king. He could have had Nathan killed for talking to him with such words and tone. As a matter of fact, many kings after David did that very thing. They killed the prophets who brought the word of the Lord forth because their pride blinded them and they refused to repent. So what stopped David from doing this? David and Nathan had a relationship. David respected Nathan and Nathan loved David. That's always the key when you are confronted with truth - having a relationship with the confronter.

> *PROVERBS 27:5-6 NKJV*
> *Open rebuke is better than love carefully concealed. Faithful are the wounds of a friend, but the kisses of an enemy are deceitful.*

When you are in a relationship based on nothing but pure love, it is not concealed. The one you are in relationship with will do whatever it takes to help you truly live the life God has in store for you. When a friend brings truth in your life and confronts you about sin, he or she is a faithful friend indeed. They are the kind of friend that will last. Your enemies are the ones you will tell you how awesome you are, when you are not. Your friends will tell you the truth in a spirit of love. So Nathan confronted David with harsh words but in a spirit of love, and David responded correctly.

In the next chapter we will explore the topic of repentance and how important it is to restoration. True repentance will not happen and we will never move to true breakthrough if we do not accept personal responsibility. Abraham Lincoln said, "You cannot escape the responsibility of tomorrow by evading it today." We have somehow been programmed that we can say or do whatever we want and there will be no consequences for our actions. There are consequences for our actions. One thing I have learned through many missteps is that you earn respect and trust by owning up to your actions, taking the full blame and the full weight of personal responsibility.

Chapter 3
Brokenness &
Repentance

Take a brief moment and visit getupbook.com to view Chapter Video 3. This video teaches about repentance and how it can truly change our life.

Falling Rocks

> *1 John 1:9 NIV*
>
> *If we confess our sins, he is faithful and just and will forgive us our sins and purify us from all unrighteousness.*

One of my favorite comedians has a bit in his stand-up act where talks about goofy things he has seen while driving. He mentioned a sign that said, "Blasting Zone - Falling Rocks." The punch line was, "Shouldn't that sign say, 'Road Closed'?!" I could not agree more. Common sense would say that road is definitely not safe to take!

What we need to understand is that this is exactly what God asks us to do. He wants us to take the road of repentance, with rocks all around us, in order for us to reach the road of restoration. It is not the "safe" road because we abandon all self-preservation in order to be free.

The teaching of Jesus has transformed and continues to renew the hearts of and minds of men and women throughout eternity. One particular teaching He gave us that constantly reminds me of the topic of brokenness is when he is telling a parable to a crowd and within the crowd are a bunch of religious people. In Matthew 21:44, after telling the parable, he makes this remarkable statement: "And whoever falls on this stone will be broken; but on whomever it falls, it will grind him to powder." Jesus was talking to the religious leaders, telling them that it was about time to repent and get humble or they would not only be humbled, but they would be crushed and die in their pride.

I always take this kind of language from Jesus right to heart. I don't want to be crushed. I would much rather be broken voluntarily. Do not get me wrong, they both hurt, but being crushed is much more humiliating than being broken.

I may lose some of the ladies on this next example, but humor me. It is kind of like when you and a buddy take turns punching each other in the arm. I know, it sounds like a dumb thing to do, but hey - we're guys, it's what we do. When you trade punches you know it is coming, you know it is going to hurt, but you take it. You club each other back and forth until someone gives up. You can usually take the punch because you know it is coming.

Then there is the other kind of punch: the sucker punch. Those really hurt, not because they have so much power but because you are not expecting it. It comes out of nowhere and just catches you off guard! I have seen one-punch knockouts because of a sucker punch.

That is how I see the difference between being broken and being crushed. When you choose brokenness, you voluntarily throw yourself on Jesus so He can break down your pride and sin for the sole purpose of building you back up in His likeness. Being crushed? Well not so much. That comes out of nowhere and catches you out of the blue! The sooner you realize you have been crushed and accept the humbling process, the sooner you can get up and move forward. One is voluntary and the other is not. Both are extremely painful, but both can produce the same results if we are willing to walk through the process.

"When God wants to do an impossible task, He takes an impossible man, and He crushes him."

-Alan Redpath

This quote speaks volumes. It tells us that God will take the things that get us jacked up and use those characteristics for His glory! God has intended for us to do great and mighty things.

> **In order for us to do great things for Him, we must stop doing selfish things for us.**

In the book of Daniel, chapter eleven in the last part of the thirty-second verse, He says, "but the people who know their God shall be strong, and carry out great exploits." God wants us to know Him. He longs for us to know Him not because He is lonely and needs company, but because He wants us to do great things! In order for us to do great things for Him, we must stop doing selfish things for us.

● ● ●

The Gift of Repentance & The Kindness of God

Repentance is an important Biblical topic that is taught in most churches, but rarely practiced and rarely taught correctly. The popular belief looks something like this: we "repent" on Sunday for what we did on Saturday and plan on doing again on Monday! We get the idea of being "sorry" for our sin. We feel guilty for what we have done, and we throw up a half-hearted prayer asking for forgiveness and saying, "Sorry, God." Basically we offer an anemic spiritual apology.

By and large, that is what most Christians believe repentance is. It is not. That is emotional nonsense that will pave the wide road straight to hell! Repentance is much more than apologizing for sin. God doesn't want an apology – He wants our hearts!

> ROMANS 2:4 NIV
>
> *Or do you show contempt for the riches of his kindness, tolerance and patience, not realizing that God's kindness leads you toward repentance?*

Repentance is a turning away from sin and a complete abandonment to our selfish desires. It is when we forsake every evil desire rather than forsaking God. Not because we fear hell or the earthly consequences of our actions, but because of our love for Him! God leads us into repentance. He gives us a beautiful opportunity to examine our lives and realize that without Him and His overwhelming forgiveness through Jesus Christ, we are lost. Repentance is a gift from God. Jesus started his ministry with the message of repentance and ended it with the same message.

Repentance, like worship, is a lifestyle and not an event. We think repentance is reveling in the dirt like a slimy no-good worm, as if the more self-deprecating we act, the more humble we are or more repentant we seem. It is not that either! Repentance is an honor and a privilege to look towards a loving God and reaffirm our love and service to Him on a daily basis. It is getting to recognize God as the Creator and having a proper perspective of ourselves as the created.

Personally and corporately, we need a radical revival of repentance and we need to aggressively seek the gift of repentance, like a child does when he sees a bunch of gifts on Christmas morning wrapped under the tree. God is a giver. He is a good God and a giver of gifts and repentance should be considered as such!

Let's look at how Paul describes the difference between feeling emotionally bad about sin and discovering the gift of repentance.

> 2 CORINTHIANS 7:8-10 NIV
>
> *Even if I caused you sorrow by my letter, I do not regret it. Though I did regret it–I see that my letter hurt you, but only for a little while–yet now I am happy, not because you were made sorry, but because your sorrow led you to repentance. For you became sorrowful as God intended and so were not harmed in any way by us. Godly sorrow brings repentance that leads to salvation and leaves no regret, but worldly sorrow brings death.*

Repentance is the intention of God. Paul specifically communicates that God intends for us to be sorrowful over our sin. He built us with emotions and hardwired us to feel emotions. He uses those emotions with the help of the Holy Spirit to lead us towards repentance. Repentance is not just sitting there depressed about your sin. If that were the case, Christians would be the most depressed and suicidal people on Earth (although it seems like some are anyway)! As a Christian, you are going to feel guilty about sin. It is what you do with that feeling that distinguishes between 'godly sorrow' and 'worldly sorrow.' Godly sorrow leaves no regret. If you are still regretting the sins you have done in the past, you are still operating in worldly sorrow, and you need to get up out of it because it leads to death.

Repentance is a gift of kindness from God. God loves us so much He sent Jesus to die in our place. Stop and reread that sentence just one more time. He loves you. He wants the very best for you.

One of the most interesting things about what God spoke to David through Nathan is found in 2 Samuel 12:8. This blows my mind because it shows a level of depth of the generosity and goodness of God.

> 2 SAMUEL 12:8 NKJV
>
> *I gave you your master's house and your master's wives into your keeping, and gave you the house of Israel and Judah. And if that had been too little, I also would have given you much more!*

Are you kidding me? This is unreal! This is God's love shown in a huge way! God was basically saying, "David, all you had to do was ask. If you wanted more, I would have given it to you." The heart of God here blows me away. God loves us so much that His heart is to always give; His heart is to always bless.

> **Even in the midst of our sin, God loves us!**

Even in the midst of our sin, God loves us! If there is something we are unsatisfied with, we just go to God and talk to Him about it. He wants to be our source. He wants us to rely on Him. God never wants us to have to seek outside of the all-providing relationship we have in Him for anything. He wants to be our everything. The problem appears when we think we know what we want and our fleshly, selfish desires pollute our thinking. Then we start to seek outside the bounds of God's relationship with us and we get into all kinds of evil. God is just waiting for us to run to Him. His Father's heart is beckoning us to trust Him in everything.

Consequences vs. God's Love vs. Punishment

> *2 SAMUEL 12:9-14 NIV*
>
> *Why did you despise the word of the Lord by doing what is evil in his eyes? You struck down Uriah the Hittite with the sword and took his wife to be your own. You killed him with the sword of the Ammonites. Now, therefore, the sword will never depart from your house, because you despised me and took the wife of Uriah the Hittite to be your own.*
>
> *This is what the Lord says: 'Out of your own household I am going to bring calamity upon you. Before your very eyes I will take your wives and give them to one who is close to you, and he will lie with your wives in broad daylight.*
>
> *You did it in secret, but I will do this thing in broad daylight before all Israel.' Then David said to Nathan, "I have sinned against the Lord." Nathan replied, "The Lord has taken away your sin. You are not going to die. But because by doing this you have made the enemies of the Lord show utter contempt, the son born to you will die."*

The severity of David's consequences seem to outweigh the severity of the sin he committed. As I read the things that David's lineage was to endure because of his actions, I felt it was a bit over the top. God quickly corrected my thinking though when I started to think about how David's actions affected Uriah and his family. The actions of our sin have a ripple effect. God forgives what we do, but that does not stop the waves from rolling and the storm of pain from hitting the shores of the lives of those who surround us. Sowing and reaping. Action and reaction. Call it what you want, but the truth remains that there will be consequences for our sin. Likewise, there will be results for repentance.

This is where we need to jump off the narrative of David for a moment. We must be crystal clear on the context of these verses. If not, we will believe something about God's actions and His character that just is not true. God dealt with David in the old covenant context. According to the Law of Moses, because David killed Uriah the Hittite, there was a life that needed to be taken (Exodus 21:12). So God spoke through the prophet that instead of David dying for his sin, the baby conceived in David's sin would die.

I know. Harsh.

The thing we need to understand about God – or try to understand – is that God is pure love, but He is also pure justice. He could not violate His own law! We cannot fathom the amount of pain God must have felt to see that baby die, nor can we fathom the amount of pain He must have felt when His own son Jesus was killed for our sin.

This is where our situation differs from David's. It's Jesus. Jesus is the reason we do not experience the punishment of God. Jesus established the new covenant for us, so that when we sin (that's right, not 'if' but 'when'), we experience grace and mercy rather than anger and wrath.

> We seem to confuse the punishment of God with the consequences of sin.

So God is not in the business of doling out punishment. He is in the restoration business. God does not punish us; we punish us! We seem to confuse the punishment of God with the consequences of sin. Sin being exposed is an act of love that God allows in our lives. The consequences of those things are all on us. We must recognize the difference between the things that we have brought on ourselves, which are consequences, and the punishment of God. The punishment of God is something we have never seen in our lifetime – and never want to see. We can read how God punished nations in the Old Testament before Jesus appeared on the earth. It was truly brutal. We ought to be thanking God daily that because of Jesus we do not experience the full wrath of God! Instead we experience His grace, goodness, and His mercy.

• • •

Leading by Example

As a leader of our family, ministry, or company, the greatest impact we will have is by our example. How we live our life will be the true test of the impact we make in the world around us. We can teach what we know, but we reproduce who we are. This will apply to every area of our life and leadership. I have found that when I just admit what I have done wrong, my wife and kids have a deeper respect for me than if I just put up a facade as if I am just fine when they know full well that I am not!

> Speaking the truth will always earn us respect.

We see it all the time with politicians and celebrities who make some really bad moral decisions. The ones who admit what they have done, take responsibility for it, and work towards making it right are the ones for whom we have a deeper respect. Speaking the truth will always earn us respect. David's example and response to being confronted with the truth of his sin is excellent and was a perfect picture of what our response should look like.

> 2 SAMUEL 12:13 NKJV
> So David said to Nathan, "I have sinned against the Lord."

This is such a short verse, but within this one line are some powerful truths. Let's look at two. The first truth is that David sinned against God. When we sin, it is against God alone. We do not sin against anyone but the Lord. We may hurt our spouse with what we have done. We may break our trust with our employer with our actions. But we must understand the sin issue is between God and us. The one Person we say we love the most in our lives is the one Person that we have sinned against.

The second truth of this verse is in David's example of true and genuine repentance. There is an honest, transparent, and open admission of guilt, not just because we got caught, but because we do not want to carry the weight that guilt and shame bring with holding back the truth. We admit we have sinned because we truly do want freedom. After talking with people who have been through the restoration process and from my own experience, most have acknowledged that at some point they wanted to "get caught" and wanted the truth to come out. It is as if there is a sigh of relief when they do not need to carry around these secrets anymore. They no longer need to allow their conscience to be singed to the point of insensitivity.

In most recovery programs, the first step to finding and getting help is admitting you have a problem that has gotten out of control. If a person cannot fully admit they have a problem, the process of restoration will be ineffective at best. I have found that people respect us more when we do not beat around the bush. When we fully admit what we have done, we have already started gaining trust and respect that was once lost.

• • •

The Heart of the Issue

> 2 CORINTHIANS 5:17 NKJV
>
> *Therefore, if anyone is in Christ, he is a new creation; old things have passed away; behold, all things have become new.*

At the heart of the issue is the heart. The external actions of a person who seems to genuinely repent may be dramatic. There may be lots of crying and snotting, there may be a bunch of promises to change, there may be a lot of external trappings of repentance... but the true test of repentance is action. God knows our heart, but people will not see it until we live it.

> God knows our heart but people will not see it until we live it.

When there is a breaking of our hearts for what we have done, and there is a breaking of our wills for what we want, it is at that point we find our hearts are changed. God wants us to be new; the Holy Spirit is in us to regenerate our hearts.

> L∪κε *6:43-45 NKJV*
>
> *For a good tree does not bear bad fruit, nor does a bad tree bear good fruit. For every tree is known by its own fruit. For men do not gather figs from thorns, nor do they gather grapes from a bramble bush. A good man out of the good treasure of his heart brings forth good; and an evil man out of the evil treasure of his heart brings forth evil. For out of the abundance of the heart his mouth speaks.*

Jesus lays it out very clearly here. He shows us that repentance and restoration is not a checklist of things we must do. In fact, it is always going to be an issue of the heart. Our lives and our restoration will be birthed out of the good in our hearts. How we get up will depend on our heart condition.

Heart Disease

The condition of our heart before God is illustrated perfectly through how we take care of our physical heart. Physical heart disease is caused by fatty material and plaque building up on the arteries, causing the flow of blood to slow and even stop. This usually will result in a heart attack unless something changes. The comparison to our spiritual heart is astounding to me. Like physical heart disease, in order to overcome spiritual heart disease we need to watch the build up of things that can cease the flow of life to our hearts. Offenses can build up. Resentments can build up. Things that others can do or say can be the spiritual fat that we allow into our life, and it can clog up the life-giving flow of the Spirit of God!

Lifestyle changes can help beat spiritual heart disease. Changing the diet of what we watch, listen to, and read can help the restoration process immensely. This next verse has become a life verse for me. I take it dead seriously.

>Proverbs 4:23 NKJV
>
>"Keep your heart with all diligence,
>For out of it spring the issues of life."

I also love how the New Living Translation puts it…

>"Guard your heart above all else,
>for it determines the course of your life."

This is a good reminder to monitor our spiritual diet. We have all heard the saying, "Garbage in, garbage out." It is a simple but true statement. What we allow in our lives will eventually become what we produce in our lives.

> What we allow in our lives will eventually become what we produce in our lives.

Religious people seem legalistic and narrow-minded because they get all hung up on 'secular' music or rated 'R' movies. It is unfortunate, because they are known for what they are against rather than what they are for, without ever explaining why they are against it in the first place! The reason behind not listening to a certain style of music or watching a certain movie is because simply put, it is not helpful. The media intake in our lives may not necessarily be sin, but it may not necessarily be good for our heart condition either. Paul was speaking to the Corinthian church about the grace we have in Christ when he said in 1 Corinthians 6:12, "Everything is permissible for me – but not everything is beneficial."

In my experience, when I listen to a certain style of music or watch a certain TV show or movie that does not glorify God, thoughts usually come into my mind that may dishonor God, my family, and the people I care about most. This is where the war needs to be won. If I continue to allow those thoughts to just run rampant in my mind, they will become an idea, which will become a desire, which will become, in my case, an obsession which will eventually result in an action that will put my whole life at risk! This is why it is so important to be diligent in guarding our hearts.

Another area I monitor is my social media stream. Facebook, Twitter, and the blogosphere are all areas that can be helpful, but can also turn negative and straight up nasty in a millisecond! I try and pay attention to and follow people who are positive and will build my spirit. I like the aspect of reliable critique from social media, but I don't let it define my attitude or me. As technology continues to be developed there will be more opportunities for media intake. We must be careful to monitor this and maybe even turn it off for a season, especially in the process of restoration.

Eating healthy spiritual meals is vital to maintaining heart health. This goes back to the idea of having a spiritual growth plan. Reading our Bible, praying, fasting, going to church, journaling or blogging, listening to sound Bible teachers via podcasts or teaching media, and talking with friends in a small group about what God is doing in our life – these are all ways to help us eat healthy meals and get us on a healthy spiritual diet.

● ● ●

Do a One-Eighty

It is necessary to reiterate that repentance is about action. It is about making a clean break and going the opposite direction from the way we were once going. Growing up as a skater kid, a one-eighty was the most basic move you could learn. Whether you were street skating or skating on a vert ramp, the one-eighty was the easiest but most essential move to learn, because the other tricks build off of it. If you rode a skateboard you had to do a one-eighty, or else you probably were not going to be very good at riding it.

As a Christian, doing a one-eighty is essential to living for God and absolutely vital to the process of restoration. If there is some money you need to return, do it. If there is a relationship you need to end, do it. If there is something you need to tell your spouse, get it done. If there is someone you need to forgive, forgive them already. Repentance is about doing a one-eighty. If there is something you need to do a one-eighty on, seek out a pastor at your church or a godly counselor and talk with them about the best way to do it. Regardless of how you get it done, get it done. Do a one-eighty.

Living in Forgiveness

We need to note one important thing: we live in the forgiveness of God. When we repent, God forgives us. The Bible says in Psalm 103:12, "As far as the east is from the west, so far has He removed our transgressions from us." In Micah 7:19 He says, "our sins are thrown into the depths of the sea," implying that something at the bottom of the ocean will never see the light of day! Completely forgotten!

This is where we need to live. Who are we to bring up what God has forgiven? If He has forgiven us, then we need to forgive us. Forgiving ourselves is imperative to walking in forgiveness. Depending on what you have to get up from, there may be people in your life who are not ready to forgive you, but that has no bearing on the forgiveness of God. Jesus died so you could have the assurance of forgiveness.

> *ROMANS 8:1*
>
> *There is therefore now no condemnation to those who are in Christ Jesus, who do not walk according to the flesh, but according to the Spirit.*

Condemnation can come from many different avenues and in many different ways. The most common way is through our own thought life. We need to know that because God has forgiven us and because Jesus died a torturous death on a Roman cross, we have no right to drudge up our sin and wallow in self-pity or deny ourselves the great destiny that God has planned out for us.

> We should never allow anybody else make us feel inferior or not worthy of forgiveness.

Likewise we should never allow anybody else make us feel inferior or not worthy of forgiveness. They don't have the right to do that to us and we shouldn't afford it to them either.

For years I allowed shame and guilt to keep me out of conversations and relationships that I knew I could add value to because I felt as if I was not good enough. I felt like everybody knew my sin and because of the sin in my life, I believed my words no longer carried any weight. I lived in false assumptions that I "just knew" people had about me. Nothing could have been farther from the truth. Nobody "knew" jack!

That's how condemnation works. It may be as blatant as telling you, "You're no good. How could God forgive you after what you have done? These people know you are a fake, phony Christian! Who are you to offer help? You can't even run your own life right much less help people with theirs!" These were the thoughts I wrestled with. The reality was only a few people knew about my sin and the process of restoration I was in. Jesus was perfect. The reason He died for us is because we have all fallen short of God's standard (Romans 3:23) and God's standard is perfection. If the standard of being in ministry or serving God were perfection then nobody would be teaching, preaching, serving in any church or ministry, or trying to help anybody! For me to offer help to someone else is the very nature of God working through me to try and improve the lives of people around me.

Condemnation is a sneaky booger. Again, it may be blatant and "in your face," but most of the time it is not. After I started recognizing those full-on mental attacks, I would fight through them. After awhile I noticed the more subtle attacks of condemnation. The enemy would start to play on my insecurities. For example, someone would say something that related to an area of weakness of mine, or an area of ministry I wanted to be doing, I would immediately feel defensive or get all bowed up and show everybody how "spiritual" I was. In fact, the person who said something did not even mean anything by it. Condemnation makes you think it is all about you and that everybody is talking bad about you. It is almost like a self-deprecating form of pride!

Condemnation can work its way into how we perceive our situation, those around us, our relationship with the Lord, and our how we see ourselves. If we do not recognize condemnation, we can filter everything in our lives through its lens. The area of self-perception is one in which I had some major rewiring to do. I knew I had a call to ministry, to preaching, and to leading people, but because of the sin I committed I was not doing those things anymore. I was in the marketing department doing graphic design.

Working at a huge church and having a background in ministry for as long as I did, this made the process of restoration very hard. The reason is that I could see problems other ministries were having or were going to have a mile away and I knew how to fix them. I had the solution and I could help them! But it did not matter. It was not my area of ministry and nobody even asked for my opinion. This was very humbling for me. Most people on staff with me had no clue that I had been a pastor for years or went to Bible College. People would be having big meetings and conversations about how lives were being changed, and there I was, just 'the graphic guy' piddling around on the computer. I had countless days of feeling defeated, unneeded, and like what I did throughout the day just did not matter in light of eternity.

> This is the season when we learn our value is not based on what we do but who we are.

This is the paradox of restoration. This is the season when we learn our value is not based on what we do but who we are. So who was I really? I was a son of God, a loving husband, and a tender father to my two beautiful daughters. I was pastoring my family the way God intended. I was fulfilling the first priority. Really, what else is there? So actually, what I did throughout the day really did matter in light of eternity. What you do matters too!

So, who are you? Are you stuck in condemnation? Is your self worth based on what you do or have done? Or is it based on who God says you are? We must answer these questions and recognize where we are, because our self worth cannot come from external sources and stimulations. It must come from the truth of God's word and the power of the Holy Spirit that resides on the inside of us.

> *PSALM 103:1-5 NKJV*
> *A Psalm Of David.*
>
> *Bless the Lord, O my soul; And all that is within me, bless His holy name!*

*Bless the Lord, O my soul,
And forget not all His benefits:*

*Who forgives all your iniquities,
Who heals all your diseases,*

*Who redeems your life from destruction,
Who crowns you with lovingkindness and tender mercies,*

*Who satisfies your mouth with good things,
So that your youth is renewed like the eagles.*

Even with all that David experienced, he knew God's forgiveness. He lived there. Our job is not to "feel" forgiven, our job is to receive forgiveness and walk it out. That means we put the shame, guilt, accusation, and sin behind us. It is not that we forget about it, because I feel it serves as a great reminder of who we are without God. It is that we don't allow it to rule and reign in our hearts.

> **If we allow the failure of yesterday into the thought life of today it will surely ruin the success of our tomorrow.**

If we allow the failure of yesterday into the thought life of today it will surely ruin the success of our tomorrow. We must meditate and ponder on scriptures like these. These are the words of life to our dying souls. These are the very life-giving words of God that we so desperately need.

Chapter 4
Developing Self-Control & Accountability

Take a brief moment and visit getupbook.com to view Chapter Video 4. This video is about self-control and accountability; two extremely important aspects in our restoration process.

Controlled Chaos

> GALATIANS *5:22-23 ESV*
>
> *But the fruit of the Spirit is love, joy, peace, patience, kindness, goodness, faithfulness, gentleness, self-control; against such things there is no law.*

The idea of controlled chaos is a conundrum. Chaos is uncontrollable. The whole purpose of control is to not have chaos. Controlling chaos is next to an impossible feat. But it is precisely what we do when we start to learn and practice restraint.

When we first get into the process of restoration, it seems like chaos is all around us. Our thoughts seem out of control. Whatever sin got us here still seems to be hanging on, those closest to us seem to be the farthest away, and finding freedom from sin seems like we are climbing a mountain in a pair of flip flops! It all seems pretty overwhelming. That pet sin of ours has hung around so long, it seems like a piece of us. The truth is, it is not a part of you. The restoration process is not just possible; it will happen if you keep moving forward. The first step to controlling chaos is actually giving it a try.

In this chapter we will talk about some concepts that will help us understand the motive of self-control, the community of self-control, and the practicality of self-control. Let's begin with the motive of self-control and restoration.

Love & Law

2 Corinthians 3:4-6 NKJV

And we have such trust through Christ toward God. Not that we are sufficient of ourselves to think of anything as being from ourselves, but our sufficiency is from God, who also made us sufficient as ministers of the new covenant, not of the letter but of the Spirit; for the letter kills, but the Spirit gives life.

This passage of scripture seems like one of those "deep theological truths" that only the Christian MVP's get to understand. In reality, it is very simple. Paul is letting us know that through God and God alone we are sufficient. We cannot follow enough rules and regulations to be OK with Him and experience restoration. He even implies that we will die trying to keep all the rules; our life must come through the Spirit and we must live from the inside out. All the rule keeping in the world is not going to help us gain any spiritual ground with God.

Restoration comes from God alone. It happens in our hearts, and is lived out in our actions. We cannot "fake it until we make it" on this one. There ain't no fakin' this! There is not a checklist big enough that will foster the kind of restoration that God wants to do in our hearts.

In the process of restoration, there is a tendency to want to make a "to-do" list, a checklist that proves to us and everyone else around us that we are making progress. We want them to know we are seeing a counselor and are getting better. We want them to know we are going to recovery meetings. We want them to know we are attending and serving at church. We feel that if we could prove we are making all these external strides, we are being restored and moving on into our destiny.

> We could be doing all the right things and at the center of it, we are not even close to being the person we are trying to portray to those around us.

We could be doing all the right things and at the center of it, we are not even close to being the person we are trying to portray to those around us. It is like we are following all the rules without even knowing why.

I can still recall my first few months in the restoration process. The expectations I laid out for myself seemed very rigid and legalistic. There were a lot of rules, regulations, and restraints – a boatload of "can do's & can't do's." I was checking off every list imaginable. I attended my "90 in 90," which in Narcotics Anonymous means that right out of treatment you need to attend 90 NA meetings in 90 days. And I did! Not only that, I went to Celebrate Recovery meetings, took drug tests, installed porn accountability software on my computer, met with a counselor once a week, got a sponsor and called him everyday, went to every church service I could, and the list went on and on and on.

I was running around doing a bunch of activity, and I had to constantly ask myself why was I doing this. What was the motive of my heart? Did I really want freedom, or did I just not want to lose the life I was accustomed to? Or did I just want to impress the people around me and make them think I was OK now? Restoration will test your heart. It will reveal the motive of why we do what we do.

Then it hit me like a freight train. I am doing this because I love God and I will do anything to be free. Whatever it takes, that is what I will do. That is when the Holy Spirit dropped this scripture about the law in 2 Corinthians in my heart. The reason there were all of these expectations laid out for me is not because someone wanted me to trip up and catch me slipping.

> I am doing this because I love God and I will do anything to be free.

It was not because I had to prove how good I was. Not because I just had to check off a list of rules and regulations. It was because these people love me and want the very best for my family and me! It is the difference between "the letter of the law and the Spirit of the law." If I just try to live up to all of these expectations at an external level without really allowing them to change and penetrate my heart, it is worthless. It is religious, legalistic activity!

On the other hand, if I understand that the Spirit of the law is love and the motive of it is love and that God is pure love, well now we are talking! Now I know that this is not just a list of rules, but it is a formula of love that has been implemented in my life. I would be a fool to pass it up! It is the difference between religion and relationship. Religion is striving to live by a set of rules for the sake of keeping rules. Relationship is living a pure life because we do not want to break God's heart.

● ● ●

Kick Him in the Goads!

> Acts 9:3-6 NKJV
>
> *As he journeyed he came near Damascus, and suddenly a light shone around him from heaven. Then he fell to the ground, and heard a voice saying to him, "Saul, Saul, why are you persecuting Me?"*
>
> *And he said, "Who are You, Lord?"*
>
> *Then the Lord said, "I am Jesus, whom you are persecuting. It is hard for you to kick against the goads."*
>
> *So he, trembling and astonished, said, "Lord, what do You want me to do?"*
>
> *Then the Lord said to him, "Arise and go into the city, and you will be told what you must do."*

I have read through Acts a number of times, but it was not until I was in the restoration process that I noticed that bit about "kicking goads." What's a goad and why is hard to kick them? After some research and looking at a couple other translations, I learned that a goad is another word for "prick" or more specifically, a round sharpened, wooden stake. It is a tool that farmers would use to poke and prod an animal to get it going in the right direction. Out of sheer anger the animal would sometimes kick it and it would of course result in injury, stabbing the animal in the leg!

As I meditated that verse, I kept thinking, "That is a weird thing to say. What is the point?" (No pun intended!) "Why would Jesus say that to Paul?" Think about when you've stepped on a splinter or a thorn. It's a pretty painful experience. Now kick it up a notch (literally!) and think about not just stepping on, but kicking a thorn. Ouch! Now take another step and think about kicking a round, wooden stake.

Talk about pain! That's terrible – I get a weak stomach just thinking of the agony!

Then the Holy Spirit revealed it to me through my own experience. God showed me that the restoration process is similar to a goad. It pokes and prods until you start going the right direction. It is frustrating, inconvenient, irritating, and just down right painful at times. Out of sheer anger we want to kick the process and when we do kick it, we kick it right in the goads! Every time we buck up against the restorative process we just end up hurting ourselves. We have to realize the process is birthed out of love and is there to guide us in the right direction, even if hurts at times.

• • •

Your Inner Circle

This next section will help us understand the community of self-control. I know that sounds weird, almost like an oxymoron. Community and self-control. I have found that self-control can be better developed and more matured when you have a few people in your life that will help foster it. I call this the "community of self-control." These people help us stay on track. They help us reframe our temptations, thoughts, and situations. They are the closest to us and are also known as our inner circle.

> *"Natural accountability will ride on the back of un-conditional love."*
>
> -Matthew Barnett

When I was early on in my sin, I came to a place where the guilt was weighing on me so heavily that I called a friend of mine who was a

Christian. This was not someone I had a really tight relationship with because we had not talked in quite a while. I called him because I had no one to talk to – or so I thought. I called this guy up and just told him everything. Call me naive or stupid but I just needed to get this stuff off my chest.

Well, this was a bad mistake. It turned into a power play on his part and that relationship turned out to be extremely unhealthy and did more harm than good. I write this because you need to know it is of the greatest importance that we have at least one safe, healthy relationship with someone we can trust to keep their mouth shut to others, but at the same time bring truth to our life and help us see the consequences of our actions.

For David, this was Nathan. Nathan did not work for David, he was not on the payroll, they were not drinking buddies, and they were not related. Nathan was David's accountability partner. He brought forth the truth in David's life, laid out the consequences of his actions, and showed David that God still loved him, but the result of his sin will change the trajectory of his heritage for years to come! This is what real accountability looks like.

My accountability starts with the two most important relationships in my life: God and my wife. The Holy Spirit is called the helper, guide, and teacher. He has helped me in more ways than I could write about. One of the major ways I have experienced His help is when I cross the line of temptation. He gently – or sometimes harshly, depending on my level of rebellion – pokes at my heart and checks my spirit to get me to evaluate my behavior, realign it with the truth of God's word and then display the character of Jesus.

> Without the power of the Holy Spirit, all of our activity amounts to behavior modification and not true heart transformation.

He guides me in the way I should treat people and how my attitude affects the restoration process. He teaches me through the reading of His Word and how to apply what He shows me in everyday life. Without the power of the Holy Spirit, all of our activity amounts to behavior modification and not true heart transformation. The Holy Spirit is the key to restoration. We do the natural work of changing our habits and He does the supernatural work of changing our hearts.

The second relationship is key. Our spouse is the one who should be able to see right through us. They know how we are when we are sick, when we are sad, and when we are at our worst. I can honestly say that I have hurt my wife in ways I am ashamed of and could never express the regret I feel about it. The grace, mercy, and love she has shown to me could only come from God. She is the most forgiving, loving, and amazing person I know. It is my job to let her know that I will become the husband and father that God has called me to be.

As far as accountability goes, we have a very balanced relationship. There's a funny line from the movie "My Big Fat Greek Wedding" that reminds me of our relationship. It goes like this, "The husband... he is the head but the wife... she is the neck!" My wife has an innate ability to know when I am heading the wrong direction. She can turn me toward where I need to go. She does not do it in a nagging, controlling, or demanding way, but in a way that encourages and helps me. After all, she is my helpmate.

Another thing I am careful of is how I express my weakness and failures to her. I always communicate honestly when I am feeling weak, tempted, or have failed, but *how* we communicate those things to each other is essential to the health of our relationship. There are some areas in which she encourages me to talk to someone else, and knowing that we have the freedom to communicate to each other in this way makes all the difference in the world. It was not an overnight success and we are not even close to having it perfected, but we are continuing to work on this area of communication in our marriage. I have found the more we do this, the closer we become, and the more respect we have for each other.

If you are not married then there needs to be someone in your life that you can talk to openly and honestly. There needs to be a close relationship you have that can bring you truth. The first place I would start is at the local church. Look for a pastoral staff member that may be willing to take you on as an accountability partner. If that does not work out, a small group leader might be the way to go. There are also Celebrate Recovery programs that are available nationwide. Chances are that there is some type of church or organizations in your city that you can plug into that will help you get on the road to restoration. It is just a matter of desire.

If we want these types of accountable relationships, we have to seek them out. Somebody is not going to show up on your doorstep, ring the doorbell, and present you with a business card that says, "Hi, I'm your new accountability partner!" It is just not going to happen that way. We have to be proactive in the area of accountability. My belief is that God has provided the relationship we need when it comes to this area; it is just a matter of recognition. We may not have to seek this person out. They may already be in our life and we just need to recognize them as being qualified to be part of our inner circle.

Intentional Accountability

Accountability does not just happen. It takes time and sometimes determination to get the right people in your life. No matter what, it is important that we have a plan of intentional accountability. Think about it: the enemy comes at you with guns blazing, trying to steal every blessing in your life, kill your destiny and purpose, and ultimately kill you!

> *John 10:10 NKJV*
>
> *The thief does not come except to steal, and to kill, and to destroy. I have come that they may have life, and that they may have it more abundantly.*

The devil has a plan for your life just like God does! So my answer was to put together a plan of attack as well. It was a strategic plan that I feel God gave me as a guide to walking out restoration. My plan and your plan are probably going to look different. Different strategies win different battles. As I shared in group therapy while in treatment the plan I felt God gave me, many of the guys in my small group within treatment wanted a copy! They jokingly called it "The P90X of Recovery!" My exact plan would not work for them because our lives were all very different. Nonetheless, they saw the value of having a plan and so should you.

> **We must live with intentionality or most of our life will happen by accident.**

A plan sets us up for success. It helps us live with intentionality. We must live with intentionality or most of our life will happen by accident. One of the most tragic things a person can do is just live a bland life. We can happen to life rather than life happening to us!

> *"Your life doesn't just happen. Whether you know it or not, it is carefully designed by you."*
>
> -Stephen R. Covey

It is incredible how many people, including myself, try to live life without a plan. Even when we do not have a plan, it is still a plan. It is just not a very good plan. It is a plan not to do much because the plan does not say to do anything! When we live with a plan, we live with a sense of urgency to accomplish the plan and a clearly defined strategy that we apply with intentionality. We must take the time to put pen to paper and write out a plan of attack in order to live the destiny to which God has called us. God will give us a plan and a strategy if we take the time to develop it.

Here are some ways that you can begin to develop a plan of attack for your life:

- **Take the time to listen to Him.**
  Taking time to pray everyday and just sitting in silence listening for His voice is a practice that has served me well. It is in that time that I can focus on God and God alone. It is usually in that time I get a thought or an idea or a "check" in my spirit to do a certain thing or call a certain person.

- **Think how you can strengthen your area of weakness.**
  Whatever we are struggling with, there is a resource for help. In addition to Bible reading, invest in some books that will help you gain knowledge and understanding in

the area in which you are weak. Hosea 4:6 (NKJV) says, "My people are destroyed for lack of knowledge." Reading books, listening to teaching, and attending conferences are all ways to pump up our knowledge base.

- **Apply what you learn**
  James 1:22 (NKJV) says, "But be doers of the word, and not hearers only, deceiving yourselves." 1 Corinthians 8:1 (NKJV) says, "Knowledge puffs up." We have to see the implication of these two verses. Just gathering knowledge is not enough. We have to use that knowledge. I like to call this "wisdom." Wisdom is knowledge applied. When we use the knowledge we have gained, we apply wisdom in our lives. It is pointless to walk around like an inflated bobble-head all filled up with knowledge if we are not going to use it! That leads to pride! Knowledge is only good when you use it.

- **Share what you have learned**
  An important principle to realize is that when we teach or share what we have learned with other people, it actually solidifies the lesson in our own hearts. When we do share, it should never be with a "hey-I-know-more-than-you" attitude, but from a place of sharing about what God is doing in your life and this is what you are learning through it.

For me, I completely submerged myself in this concept of implementing a plan of attack. I made it a point to obtain every weapon I could get my hands on and make it a part of my spiritual arsenal. The first thing I did was make an appointment with a Christian counselor. I ended up seeing him once a week for the next three months, and every other week for three months after that, to talk about life, stress, marriage, addiction, calling, purpose, destiny, personality style – basically everything I needed to hash through to help get me to a place of restoration. I do not visit with him weekly anymore, but twice a year I get a "check-up," almost like an emotional and spiritual tune-up.

In addition to seeing a counselor, I established an intensive, high-accountability relationship with one of the executive pastors at my church. We knew there would be a high demand of time and energy that he would need to put in this relationship. We wanted to respect that, so we determined to have a three-month limit placed on this accountability situation. If all went according to plan, at the end of the three months a staff pastor with whom we both had great relationships would step in to be my accountability partner indefinitely. This staff pastor is still one of my accountability partners to this day. I have another guy in my life who is not a pastor, but he is a Christian who has had the same struggles with addiction, has been clean for a number of years, and still attends the same recovery program as me. I call this guy my sponsor.

So there you have it – my inner circle. This is my community of self-control. These guys, along with my wife, have helped keep me on track through a process of honest community. They have helped plant the seeds of self-control. Through the nurturing process of restoration, God has brought the increase of this fruit of the Spirit in my life. My belief is regardless of where you are, how old you are, or how mature you may think you are, we all need an inner circle of people who help keep us on track.

Genuine Accountability vs. False Accountability

Unfortunately, accountability has gotten a bad rap in recent years. We have a massive misunderstanding of what it really is. I have been in different accountability situations through the years. I have experienced the good and the bad of accountability. From my own experience, I will define the difference between genuine accountability and false accountability.

Genuine accountability:

- **Is honest, open, and transparent.**

    It is pointless to lie to your accountability partner. Honesty is the only way accountability works. Like David, we must have full disclosure on where we are or else accountability is ineffective.

- **Will only work if you work it.**

    Accountability only works if you use it. You cannot expect a hammer to drive a nail into a piece of wood by itself, just like accountability will work if it is not used. Accountability is a tool to be used, not a trophy to put on your shelf.

- **Has consequences built in.**

    There should be an agreement that if someone in the accountable relationship fails morally, there are consequences pre-outlined. Consequences are a natural part of sin and restoration. If consequences are withheld it will slow and even stop the process of restoration.

- **Is organic.**

    There has to be a natural chemistry involved in the relationship, or else every time you meet or talk it will seem awkward and forced. You can't force a relationship. It's either there or it's not. I have been in forced scenarios and in natural scenarios. From my experience, natural relationships help bring the walls down. There is an easiness about sharing your weaknesses when you are comfortable with someone.

- **Is life-giving.**
  When you walk away from an accountability meeting there should be a feeling that you are encouraged and challenged to make positive changes. There should be a known sentiment that you are progressing in the restoration process and that your accountability partner is on your side.

False accountability:

- **Is deceptive.**
  If every time you meet, nobody has any struggles or things to talk about, somebody is probably lying. Nobody is perfect. There is always something to talk about and areas for improvement. The "what-they-don't-know-won't-hurt-them" mindset does not work in accountability; it is called "sinning by omission."

- **Is controlling.**
  In this type of relationship there is a sense of blackmail with one person trying to control the other. It is a power play in which one person tries to use the consequences of failure to manipulate the other person into doing something that is not helpful to the process of restoration, but instead will personally benefit the manipulator. This usually turns very unhealthy very quickly, and I have even seen it turn volatile.

- **Has no consequences.**
  This is the opposite of control and manipulation. This type of "accountability" doesn't hold anyone accountable for real.

It is a sham. Fake. A facade. This is slacker accountability. It is having accountability just to say you have it. This is when people get together, talk about their failures, and pray for each other and nothing else happens. The next week, the same scenario. The week after that, the exact same scenario. There is never any change or transformation. Growth will never happen in this situation. Sin does have consequences and for restoration to happen and the process to be effective, consequences must be involved.

- **Is condemning.**

  When you walk away from an accountability meeting beat up, feeling like you are the scum of the earth, feeling no encouragement and hopeless, feeling like your salvation is in question, then it is a good indicator you have just been condemned. This type of relationship will never produce any good fruit. It will also be sure to cut off all honest communication because no one wants to share their weaknesses just to get beat up with them.

Accountability and accountable relationships should have built within them a culture of trust. In a culture of trust there is a clear expectation. Everybody knows if there is failure in any area, I will have the courage to admit what I have done wrong, and I will do whatever it takes to make it right and not let it happen again. It does not mean anyone ever messes up. It means when we do mess up, we admit it, accept the responsibility and consequences for our actions, repent, and move forward in our lives and in the relationship.

• • •

Soul Shepherds

> HEBREWS 13:17 NLT (MY EMPHASIS ADDED IN BOLD)
>
> *Obey your spiritual leaders, and do what they say.* ***Their work is to watch over your souls, and they are accountable to God.*** *Give them reason to do this with joy and not with sorrow. That would certainly not be for your benefit.*

Hebrews 13:17 shows us the reason we need to have people in our life to help keep us accountable. These are our soul shepherds. Ultimately, we are responsible for the decisions we make, but the scripture indicates they have a responsibility before the Lord to guide us in the right direction! They help tend to the spiritual needs we have and are equipped to help us in that time of need. These people are a blessing to us if we receive them that way.

In our independent, individualized, "you-can-have-it-your-way" culture, this is not well received. People, even Christians – sometimes especially Christians in the western world – are what the Bible calls "stiff-necked," meaning they humble themselves to nobody. They have the attitude of "Ain't nobody gonna tell me nothin'!" This is why the topic of spiritual authority is sometimes a heated discussion.

I find it very sad when people say stupid things like, "I'm accountable to God! I don't need anybody in my life!" or "Accountability isn't even biblical!" or my favorite stupid, super-spiritual term for rebellion, "I don't need a spiritual covering, God is my spiritual covering!" I've seen the lowest IQ on the Internet say something pseudo-spiritual about not having a spiritual covering and everybody takes it as gospel. In fact, it is usually birthed from a wounded heart of rebellion! Accountability, spiritual covering, and spiritual authority are not only Biblical, but they are modeled all throughout the Bible. I do not need to go into all of these relationships in depth to prove this. Instead

I have listed these Biblical examples with some scripture, and I challenge you to study them for yourself.

- God held Adam accountable. (Genesis 3:1-24)
- Jethro held Moses accountable. (Exodus 18:13-27)
- Joshua and Caleb held each other accountable. (Numbers 13)
- Nathan held David accountable. (2 Samuel 12)
- The prophets held Israel accountable. (Jeremiah, Ezekiel... virtually all of the major and minor prophets)
- Jesus held the disciples accountable. (The Gospels; Jesus is constantly challenging his disciples)
- Paul held Timothy accountable. (2 Timothy 2:22)

This is by no means an exhaustive list, but a short sampling to show that accountability is most definitely Biblical. For people who do not want spiritual authority or accountability in their life, I will just call it what it is: pride and rebellion. The original sin that plagued Lucifer is the same one that plagues us today. People will argue this all day long, but the most fruitful ministries and Christians are the ones who have and obey some type of spiritual authority in their life.

● ● ●

Some Closing Thoughts on Accountability

The Bible is pretty clear on the importance of community. The phrase "one another" appears roughly 250 times in the Bible. This means that living this Christian life alone is not God's plan and, in fact, extremely dangerous to our faith.

I watch the National Geographic channel quite a bit. The instinctive nature of a herd of gazelles is really interesting as it relates to the safety of community. Whenever we see a lion chasing after a lone gazelle, it is usually because that lion or a group of lions has made a strategic move on the herd in order to separate the gazelle, getting it by itself out in the open and away from the herd. More often than not, the animal is devoured by the pride of lions.

More often than not, that is what happens to us when we are separated from life-giving relationships. When we stay in community, we stay in safety. When we venture out alone, we are more prone to being attacked. Spiritual authority and covering is in place for our protection. These people are not God and should not be treated as such, but there should be a level of honor in place. There is something special that happens in our lives when we honor those who have gone before us and who mentor us.

> 1 JOHN 4:18 NIV
>
> *There is no fear in love. But perfect love drives out fear, because fear has to do with punishment. The one who fears is not made perfect in love.*

We walk in accountability out of a love for God, not because we fear the consequences of man. These accountability relationships should never be the driving factor in your life. If they are, they have become an idol. You are then living your life to please your accountability partners, rather than living your life to please God. Pleasing God is your motive. Do not ever get that out of whack. Pleasing God and living in freedom is the goal, not living our life in of the fear of man.

Chapter 5
Recovery & Restoration

Take a brief moment and visit getupbook.com to view Chapter Video 5. This video is about hope. It's about finding true restoration in every area of our life.

When we start out in the process of restoration, we start out from a deficit. We have made some really bad decisions and lost quite a bit. We have lost trust and respect. We have lost money and time. Some of us may have lost a job or a marriage. Regardless of our circumstance, because of sin we have all lost something. We must recover what was lost, and we will recover if we take the right steps of repentance and accountability.

After being in recovery, I started to ask myself, "When am I done recovering, and when do I experience restoration?" Recovering is great. Recovery is awesome. "Recover" means to get back what we have lost. I have found myself at the point of not only getting back what I have lost, but also receiving much more! So for me, I am experiencing restoration. Not just material things, but the intangibles such as trust, respect, and responsibility. So I am not really in recovery mode anymore. I am in restoration mode! First is recovery, and then comes restoration if we keep living the way God intended.

There is a Biblical reason why I would like to challenge staying in the recovery mindset for the rest of our lives with some scripture I have studied and some thoughts I have had after being on this journey for a while. My belief is God wants more for us than recovery; He wants restoration.

> We must move from recovery to restoration.

We must move from recovery to restoration. I believe that total freedom can be found. There are some recovery programs that have done a great deal of good that I am involved with to this very day, but a foundational belief there is one that focuses on maintenance. Their maintenance philosophy says, "I will always have this problem and it can raise its ugly head at any point in time." The program itself becomes the anchor instead of an entry point for those that need freedom. People start to live their life for the program instead of living their life to please God. So instead of the God of the program, the program becomes their god. It becomes the only avenue of freedom. In essence it becomes an idol.

Restoration is more than a program. It was not and is not free. It is expensive. It cost Jesus his life. To believe that freedom is not possible and that we must manage our sin is a slap in the face of our Savior. Jesus died to bring us freedom. It can be attained. The message of the gospel is freedom and liberty from everything that tries to drag us down to the depths of hell!

> *Isaiah 61:1 NIV (my emphasis added in bold)*
> *The Spirit of the Sovereign Lord is on me, because the Lord has anointed me to proclaim good news to the poor. He has sent me to bind up the brokenhearted, to proclaim **freedom** for the captives and **release** from darkness for the prisoners;*

COLOSSIANS *1:13-14 NLT (MY EMPHASIS ADDED IN BOLD)*

For he has rescued us from the kingdom of darkness and transferred us into the Kingdom of his dear Son, who **purchased our freedom** *and forgave our sins.*

JOHN *8:36 NKJV*
Therefore if the Son makes you free, you shall be free indeed.

None of those verses mention anything about living in recovery! Like I said, those are good programs and have helped a lot of people, including myself, but at their foundation they do not take recovery on to restoration. Those verses show us Jesus paid for our freedom with His life. He came to this earth to bring us good news and part of that good news is we don't have to live in the vicious cycle of sin for the rest of our lives. We can achieve freedom and we can learn to live life the way God intended. We can reach the point of restoration! Some might argue that I'm splitting hairs with the terminology, but for me I would rather be at a place of restoration and growth, rather than looking at my life as if I am still at a deficit of having to get back what I have lost.

Junkyard Jesus

I love the whole idea of restoration. I love seeing restoration happen. I love it so much I actually watch television shows about restoring stuff. These are things like cars, motorcycles, and antiques. The show usually goes like this: We see an old junkyard with some old beaters. It is a car graveyard. Most, if not all, of these cars are rusted out. The interior is all ripped up and there are usually rats and other animals that are living there at this point. Then we take a look under the hood, of course it is all rusted out and there are weeds actually growing out of the engine! This car needs a lot of work. There is no way it is even close to being drivable.

At that point the master fabricator shows up. This guy is the man. He has restored countless cars. He looks at this vehicle and sees what it could and should be. He sees the cherry red paint job and the chromed out wheels, he hears the roaring engine, he can smell the new interior…he already sees this thing as a beautiful muscle car. But the reality is, it is a piece of crap at the moment. The current owner cannot believe this guy is willing to pay thousands of dollars for it in this condition!

Here is the deal though: the Master fabricator sees its value. He sees what it could be and what it should be. He pays the price and now owns the hunk of junk. So he tells his boys to back up the tow truck and load it up. Now the vehicle has been recovered, but it is time to take it to the shop and start the process of restoration.

Before long this vehicle starts to take shape. They grind the car down to the bare metal. They replace the engine and transmission. The frame is cleaned up and the body goes into paint. New wiring has been done. The interior is now all brand new. Then comes the day when it is time to crank the engine. The Master fabricator has done this so many times, he has complete confidence it will start up on the first try –and it does! He looks at his crew and they celebrate, because they've taken this car from the junkyard to showroom floor.

In case you have not made the connection, that Master fabricator is Jesus. He does the same thing with us.

When is the Process Over?

Restoration doesn't happen in a day, a month, a year, or multiple years. There is no timeline. We as humans like timelines. We want to know when our favorite show is on. We want to know when the church service is over. We tap our foot standing in front of the microwave. We just love to know timelines, when things start and when things finish. We want to know when we are restored.

God doesn't work that way. He had the Israelites march around in the desert for forty years after they were delivered from Egypt because that is how long it took to learn what God was trying to teach them!

> The idea of a timeline for restoration is man's feeble attempt at putting natural limitations on a completely spiritual process.

The idea of a timeline for restoration is man's feeble attempt at putting natural limitations on a completely spiritual process. It is ridiculous to think we are restored just because we have been in the process for a year or two. That puts a timeline on God, a God who does not operate in units of time. Being restored is between God and us. Putting a timeline out there is more detrimental than anything else. Then we think if we can just jump through enough hoops and say all the right things and impress all the right people and "white-knuckle" it through a checklist of expectations, we are restored – when the whole time our hearts are in shambles! The whole time we are just painting the rusty beast rather than having it be truly restored! We could be restored in an instant or it could take years. Only God knows that answer.

A mentor once gave me an illustration of the re-entry process. He kind of put it to me like this: we want to re-enter our career, our passion, our dream, our ministry, and our life by just jumping right in and doing stuff as if nothing ever happened. But something did happen. We suffered an injury. It is as if we broke a bone and we are sitting on the sidelines with a cast on, watching everyone else play the game we desperately want to be in! After we suffer a break, there must be a healing process that occurs.

However that happens for you will be different than how it happens for me, so we cannot compare when it comes to that. In any case though, healing must happen. After you get the cast off, there is some physical therapy that must happen. Then there is some exercise that is usually pretty painful that takes place. After a while, you start to know the pressure your bone can take, and you start to learn the limits in which you can push.

It's the same with restoration. Only you know when you are ready. We can say all day long that we are ready, but deep down in our hearts we know whether we are ready or not. The time this takes, I believe, is completely up to us. We can slow the process or we can accelerate it; it is our choice. Only we know how much pressure we can handle, so we must be honest with ourselves and those around us.

● ● ●

It's Time to Get Up

>2 SAMUEL *12:19-20 NKJV*
>
>*When David saw that his servants were whispering, David perceived that the child was dead. Therefore David said to his servants, "Is the child dead?"*

And they said, "He is dead."

So David arose from the ground, washed and anointed himself, and changed his clothes; and he went into the house of the Lord and worshiped. Then he went to his own house; and when he requested, they set food before him, and he ate.

This is an interestingly rich passage of scripture. This is the response of David when he found out his son had died. In the verses before this, David was fasting, praying, and pleading with God about not having to experience the consequences of his sin. But the consequences happened anyway, as we learned earlier in 2 Samuel 12.

The scripture shows that David arose. He got up! Not only did he get up, he went, and worshiped the Lord. We must see this. This must be our response. It is time to get up wash ourselves off, let the anointing of God flow over us anew and fresh, and go worship Him!

> **The scripture shows that David arose. He got up.**

It is as if David was showing us that, even though he was grieved about what he had done, and of course he was heartbroken over the death of his son, regardless of the circumstance he was going to worship, he was going to seek God and worship Him!

Our life of personal worship will be instrumental in how we get up. Worship, particularly when we sing, has the ability to melt away all thoughts of depression and sadness. When we use a magnifying glass, it makes things bigger. When we "magnify" God in worship we are doing just that. We make Him bigger than our problems, our guilt, and our shame. All of that stuff pales in comparison to the greatness and fullness of God!

There have been some extremely dark times in my life. I can remember when I did not "feel" like worshipping God. But the beautiful thing about worship is it works whether I am feeling it or not! Another thing we need to get is that worship is for God, but the benefit is more for us than anything else. God does not have a co-dependency problem. His perception of Himself is not based on our level of worship! He is not an egomaniac just feeding off the praises of His people. He is God all by Himself. He is the beginning and the end. He was here long before us and He will be here after we are long gone! The benefit of worship is for us. When we worship God, it gives Him the opportunity to intervene in our lives because it is a truthful and humble acknowledgement of our own inconsistencies. It puts the proper perspective on us as the created and Him as the Creator.

David did not sit in his guilt. He did not wallow in self-pity. He did not allow depression to overtake his life. The psalms are clear that he had his seasons of sadness, but he did not live there. He got up. He moved on with his life. It is time we get up and worship God! When we do this, we will continue to move forward at an accelerated rate in the process of restoration.

Restoring Trust - You Are a Little Kid... Again

Trust is one of those things that takes a lifetime to build but can be destroyed in a moment of sin. Restoring it is even harder. It is harder to earn trust back than it is to build in the first place. There are myriad things to overcome. You must overcome perceptions, unforgiveness, and insecurity.

> Trust is one of those things that takes a lifetime to build but can be destroyed in a moment of sin.

These things are birthed out of broken trust and can last years. The old "time heals everything" philosophy is not true. Time heals nothing; it is what we do in that time that brings healing.

After we have broken the trust of our spouse, our employer, and/or the people in our lives, we have to come to the realization that we are like a little kid again. When my kids were very young I could not trust them to do anything right. I knew they would make a mess of just about any activity. Whether it was brushing their teeth, taking a bath, or making a bowl of cereal, I just knew there would be a mess afterwards. They were little kids; it is to be expected.

The same applies to us. We've made a mess. Some of us larger than others, but regardless of how big, the mess remains and we have to clean it up. The way we clean it up is earning trust back. As my kids got older, there were more things with which I could trust them. They proved they could handle the responsibility of brushing their teeth without making a mess. They proved they could pour a bowl of cereal without a gallon of milk being on the floor. There are bunch of things they do now that I do not even have to give second thought to, because I know they won't make a mess, and if they do, I trust they will clean it up. On the other hand, I know there are things I still cannot trust them with. My kids are not old enough to drive yet, so letting them take the car out for a spin is out of the question. I do not trust them with that yet. I am sure in a few years that trust will be instilled, but that trust has yet to be earned.

We are in the "earning phase." Every little thing we do speaks volumes to whether we are earning trust back or not. People do not want to hear how much we have changed. They have heard it before. They want to see it. They want to see us living as the person we say we want to be, as the person we say we are now. Trust takes time to earn back. Trust is also given. You cannot take trust back. It is earned, given, and received. Through little and large acts of responsibility we earn trust back. Trust can be restored but it takes time and work.

Restoring Relationships - Rebuilding the Burned Bridges

> *"The quality of your life will never rise above the quality of your relationships."*
>
> - Larry Linkous

It is vital we rebuild the burned bridges and see those relationships restored. Relationships go hand in hand with trust, and relationships are the key to a great life. Maybe we have arrived at the place in our lives where we feel we have burned every relational bridge we have ever had. Maybe it is just one bridge that you have torched. In either case, sometimes burned bridges can be rebuilt. A physical bridge takes a lot of time, work, and resources to rebuild, and the same can be said for relational bridges. You must be willing to invest everything you have into this part of the process. It may be a good idea to think about some of these people and make a list. It does not need to be exhaustive at first. It may just be a few people to start out with, but just make you sure you start.

Making amends to the people we have harmed is probably one of the most painful things we can do. We have to relive the failure again and sometimes, so do they! Before you go trying to mend every broken relationship you have ever had, it would be a good idea to discuss it with somebody in your inner circle who can help you through the process of talking to these people. Trying to make amends may do more harm than good because the people you have harmed may not have developed a scar yet. They may still be hurting from the damage you inflicted. So tread lightly in this stage of restoration.

When restoring trust and relationships, communication to those closest to you is key. Over-communicate. If you are going to the store, tell them for what and how long you will be. If you are tempted or feeling weak in an area, tell somebody about it. Do not just sit on it and think you will fight your way through. Darkness is expelled with light. Drag it into the open and tell somebody about. Get it in the light. Live in the light. Communication is one of the most underrated and underused weapons that we have in our arsenal. Just the simple act of truthfully saying how we feel or what we are tempted with can help us, move us into maturity, and absolutely pick apart the plan of the enemy on our life. It is our choice.

Restoring Vision

When I bring up the topic of vision, many people know what I am talking about and many do not. Vision has been described as "the art of seeing the impossible." I like that definition, but it is a little lofty. It is kind of exclusive, as if it is an art form you need to learn.

A mentor of mine once said, "Vision is a preferred picture of your future." That is a much easier and a more relatable definition for me.

I think we can all dream of a better life and a more preferred future than the one we are living now, one that is possible but will take some action on our part. Vision crafting and vision casting are things that every leader must learn to do and do well if they want their organization, church, business, and the people around them to succeed. That is great for corporate vision, meaning a vision for a group of people, but my focus in this section is personal vision.

> "It is a terrible thing to see and have no vision."
>
> - Helen Keller

Helen Keller was blind and deaf, yet even she knew the power of vision. Being able to see what could be and what should be. Seeing yourself as free, healthy, and whole is the goal. My prayer is that you have that picture of yourself already there. We must think of ourselves at that place.

> PROVERBS 23:7 NKJV
>
> For as he thinks in his heart, so is he.

We must realize our best thinking got us into trouble at times, so we have to renew our minds according to God's word (Romans 12:2). We have to think of ourselves as blessed, healed, whole, complete in Christ, and totally free from sin and bondage! As we think of ourselves that way, our actions tend to go that way, and we start to become that way! The opposite is true also. When we start to think of ourselves as no-good, worthless, and insignificant, then our life tends to go that way. Part of the reason why Jesus died is to redeem us from those labels! We are good because He is good. We are worthy because He is worthy. We are significant because He is significant. He has redeemed us from our past and has given us a future and a hope (Jeremiah 29:11)!

The majority of our battles and problems are birthed in our thought life. We must be on top of our game when it comes the things that we allow in our thoughts. Our life will move in the direction of our most dominant thoughts, so we need to be thinking about how we can improve the lives of those around us through the gospel of Christ. As we do that, our lives will get better too!

> HABAKKUK 2:2 NKJV
>
> *Then the Lord answered me and said: "Write the vision and make it plain on tablets, that he may run who reads it."*

The first step in restoring vision is having a vision. Pray about this. Think about what you want your life to look like and then write it down. Write down your hopes and dreams. Write down how you want your marriage to look or what your future spouse will be like. Write down every aspect of life that you can think of and the way you picture it. That is right – picture it. Remember, vision is a picture of a preferable future. For some of us, all we can picture is gloom and doom. For some of us, if we can picture just making it through the day without picking up a drug, drink, or looking at porn, that would be just great.

It does not matter where you start, but just start picturing those positive things in your mind. I am not talking about silly, temporal things like a bigger house or a new car. I am talking about being the person God called you to be!

Your vision may be something God gave you a long time ago but because of sin, life circumstance, or any other reason you have put it on the shelf and maybe never even revisited it again. It is time to dream again. As we have allowed God to shape us in the process of restoration, we can now fully engage in what He has called us to do with integrity.

> What you do in the future will not look like what you did in the past.

What you do in the future will not look like what you did in the past. It will look different because it is done with authenticity and integrity, unmarked by the grimy stain of sin. The things we accomplish in this life will now be about Him instead of about us. God does not want our fingerprints all over His glory. When we do anything in life, it should be about His glory shining through us as vessels for His good work in the earth. Our vision, our dream should always come back to building the kingdom of God or I believe it is not really a God-given dream or vision. Ultimately it is His vision, His dream for our lives. God wants to give us fulfillment in this life. He would not give us a vision or a dream of doing something for Him unless He knew we were obedient to make it happen.

"God is most glorified in us when we are most satisfied in him."

- John Piper

When we are satisfied in Him and in right standing with Him in our daily life, God is glorified. When we are operating in the purpose and calling God has laid out for us, God is glorified. When we love those closest to us and go to great lengths to love those far from Him, God is glorified. Our call is to love God, love people, and live victoriously. When we do this, God is glorified in our lives. Vision is not some mysterious thing that is just kind of "out there." God has a vision for your life and He is just waiting for you to discover and walk in it.

Restoring Purpose

I heard a quote from a national leader who had a moral failure, a man who has gotten up and is living his destiny. He said, "It's interesting that two-thirds of the healing process will come from counselors, repentance, accountability, friends and the actual process of restoration. The last third comes from when you do what you were created to do." I have found this to be so true. As I write, preach, teach, create, dream, and motivate, I realize I am living in the purpose for which God created me.

Your purpose may be very different than mine, but the principle applies to everyone who walks through the process. God's healing seems to flow faster and stronger in our lives when we are pouring out. It is the old one-liner, "If God can get it through you, He'll get it to you!" He likes to work with reservoirs, not dams! When the life-giving power of God flows into our hearts, it is not for us just to hold onto and kind of bask in. Sure, that will take place, but the whole point of God's power is to change lives. We need to take the healing, the love, the grace, and the mercy that we have been shown by Almighty God and spread it around to everyone we come in contact with.

Luke 7:47 NIV

Therefore, I tell you, her many sins have been forgiven—as her great love has shown. But whoever has been forgiven little loves little.

I've found that when we fail and are shown mercy, we become much more merciful. When we are shown grace, we become graceful. When people believe in us, it is easier to believe in people. Our purpose is wrapped up in our relationships.

> **Our purpose is wrapped up in our relationships.**

When we start doing what we feel we are called to do, it should always have a redemptive quality to it. Our purpose should begin with God's purpose. As the first page of Rick Warren's bestselling book *The Purpose Driven Life* says, "It all starts with God." Redemption is the heart of God. God is calling us to restoration and unbroken relationship with Him. We tend to drift when we lose sight of why we are here. At the broadest point in our life, our purpose is to display the redemptive work of God. As it narrows, we begin to see the specific purpose and calling in our lives.

Chapter 6
Reaching Your Destiny

Take a brief moment and visit getupbook.com to view Chapter Video 6. This video wraps up the process of Getting Up. Reaching your destiny is more of a journey than a goal.

Living Strong. Finishing Strong.

On August 29, 2004 at the 2004 Summer Olympics, one of the most unusual things happened. Vanderlei de Lima was attempting to become the first Brazilian to win a gold medal in the marathon event. He was holding a good twenty-five second lead while approaching the twenty-second mile mark when the unthinkable took place: Vanderlei was attacked out of nowhere by a spectator. The spectator grappled with and held de Lima, trying to wrestle him to the ground with obvious hopes of not letting him finish the race. At that moment another spectator helped free de Lima from his grasp so he could continue the race.

By the time this had all taken place, two other runners passed De Lima and he lost his lead. He finished third, winning the bronze medal. At the closing of the event, the International Olympic Committee awarded de Lima with a spirit of sportsmanship award and his own country named him "Brazilian Athlete of the Year." It's a very sad and unfair story but I believe we can find the redemptive value within it.

> Hebrews 12:1 NIV
>
> *Therefore, since we are surrounded by such a great cloud of witnesses, let us throw off everything that hinders and the sin that so easily entangles. And let us run with perseverance the race marked out for us*

fixing our eyes on Jesus, the pioneer and perfecter of faith.

Vanderlei de Lima is the perfect picture of how we should run our race. The Bible instructs us to throw off those things that entangle us. I would say this guy was pretty tangled up! To take it a step further, he had some help getting untangled, which speaks to me about the power of community. Without help, he may have lost the race or even worse. Who knows what would have happened if this whack job from the crowd had not been stopped from attacking him!

Vanderlei could have stopped and blamed the guy in the crowd for why he did not finish the race. He could have allowed that guy to be the reason why he did not finish first. He could have lived his whole life in bitterness and unforgiveness, blaming this guy for his life's circumstances, but he did not. He kept running. He kept moving forward. He pushed through the pain, the adversity, and the obstacles to finish his race!

So it should be with us. We must be determined to finish our race. Our race is going to look different from everybody else's, so we might as well stop looking at how we run compared to everybody else. We need to stop complaining that our hurdles are bigger than the guy in the lane beside us. It does not matter! It is our race and nobody is going to run it for us. We must be determined that regardless of whatever whack job comes running out of the crowd, no matter how tired or fatigued we may feel, or how far away the finish line looks, we will finish our race and we are going to finish strong!

● ● ●

Reaching Your Destiny

There comes a point in everybody's life when they should realize what they were put on this planet to do. This time comes at different seasons of a person's life. Some people know from a very young age what they are destined to do, and some people actually realize their destiny while they are in the thick of doing it. Some people get toward the end of their life and realize they have been doing it the whole time. Unfortunately, some people never realize it. My belief is that if you are reading this, you want to fulfill your destiny and realize your dreams.

> Jeremiah 29:11 NKJV
>
> *"For I know the plans I have for you," declares the Lord, "plans to prosper you and not to harm you, plans to give you hope and a future."*

We must realize that we are the intentional idea of a loving God. He puts us on this earth to do something great. I cannot tell you what that is. No one can. People can guide you and give you honest feedback about where your gifting is, but only you can discover your own purpose and destiny. A popular belief is that a destiny is a destination, a stationary target. Like success, though, we live in destiny. The journey we take in life is our destiny. We can't just sit back and think that because we have accomplished a bunch of goals that we are "successful," or that we have arrived at our destiny. Life, real life, is awaiting us to live it! This is it. This is what we have, so we need to get busy about living in today and fulfilling our destiny today rather than thinking someday, maybe in the "bye and bye" we will get there. We get there in the "here and now." Our destiny is today!

I alluded to the fact that some people, if not most, do not ever reach their destiny. Maybe that is you; maybe you are sitting there thinking that your destiny has passed you up. It is just not true. I do not believe you can ever cancel or abort your destiny. I do believe through a life of continual sin and selfishness that we can postpone it and put it off, but I believe it is always there awaiting us to walk in and fulfill it. It is our choice as to what we will do with today.

> *"Go confidently in the direction of your dreams.*
> *Live the life you have imagined."*
>
> *-Henry David Thoreau*

Dust that old dream off. Get it off the shelf and begin to think about how you can do what God has called you to do. Now that you understand God is not impressed by what you do, but rather He's building who you are, it is time to start doing. We get it flipped and twisted think that if we can do enough, we are living our destiny. Our destiny will flow from who we are and will result in what we do.

> **Our destiny will flow from who we are and will result in what we do.**

When we start working for our destiny rather than allowing it to flow from who we are, then we have to question our motives for why we are doing what we are doing. Many times, our life is a result of who we are. As we walk out the process of restoration, God will give us vision and a preferred picture of the future for us to fulfill, but we will only fulfill it if we are being who He has called us to be.

• • •

Promotion Will Happen... In His Time

Psalms 75:6-7 KJV

For promotion comes neither from the east, nor from the west, nor from the south. But God is the judge: he puts down one, and sets up another.

This verse is one that I have wrestled with for years and still do to this day. It is not that I doubt it or do not believe it; it is the fact that it is truth. It is a hard truth for me to accept because marketing is part of my gift mix. I was born and raised in a self-promoting generation where everybody can be a reality star or an Internet phenom. We live in a place in time where self-promotion is the only way to get ahead, and being self-absorbed is a natural characteristic of success. Not to mention – although I will – I wrestle with immense pride, an unhealthy amount of self-love, and a sometimes overwhelming insecurity. That means I feel the need to drive the conversation back to what I am doing, what I am about, and what God is doing "through" me, when in fact, it is all a work of the flesh! So this verse lays it down, puts things in perspective. It shows that life is not about me and it is not about my destiny, but it is about God and His destiny for my life.

When true God-promotion happens, no one can stop it except for a two-part equation...us and God. We can stop it because of stupid decisions, such as willfully entering into sin no matter what form it takes. Whether it is pride, sexual sin, drug or alcohol abuse, whatever sin takes place, the second part of the equation will happen and God "puts us down" as the verse indicates.

> I believe the level of restoration and healing that takes place in our hearts will determine the level of influence that is regained.

My opinion is that God is completely over people embarrassing the name of Jesus and His church. He will remove our platform of influence for a season. I believe the level of restoration and healing that takes place in our hearts will determine the level of influence that is regained. When and if that level of influence is regained, it is more solid, more stable, and the people we are leading are more secure, knowing they not only are following a leader who knows where they have been but also knows the redemptive power of God.

• • •

Congratulations, You're Gifted... Still!

After watching the Grammy Awards every year, I am always reminded of the verse Romans 11:29.

> ROMANS 11:29 AMP
>
> For God's gifts and His call are irrevocable. [He never withdraws them when once they are given, and He does not change His mind about those to whom He gives His grace or to whom He sends His call.]

God is so in love with us that He gives us gifts, callings, talents and opportunities even though we screw up. To take it a step further, we do not even have to acknowledge Him for these gifts. We do not even have to thank the Giver of those gifts to get to use them. He just creates us that way. Of course, it is up to us to honor God with those gifts and hone those talents to become better at them, but it blows my mind that they are freely given in the first place. We all have gifts and talents. Every. Single. One of us.

I guess while watching the Grammy Awards, I have a sense of sadness because I am watching all this amazing talent being used in a temporal, self-gratifying way. Of course, I always go introspective when I find myself thinking that way, hoping to not be judgmental of others whilst I am a walking plank-eye. So it made me wonder, "Do I glory in the gifting on my life or do I give God the glory for the gifting on my life?"

First of all, I know it sounds kind of arrogant to say you are gifted, but it is really not if you approach it in the right way. Humility is knowing who you are before a holy God. Without God I can do nothing that really amounts to anything. But with God I can do all things (Phil. 4:13). So to recognize and acknowledge the God-given gift is a good thing. To thank the gift Giver and use it for Him is a great thing! But to think, for even one second, that we are the owner of the gift is when we get into pride and arrogance and that is a very bad thing.

We have to understand that we are stewards of the gift of God on our lives and we will be held accountable one day for how we used the gift God entrusted to us. The next time we have an opportunity, let's really thank God for the use of His gift on our life. No matter how bad we screw up, God's gift remains on our life; it is His love and His grace. God's gifting is not going away.

● ● ●

Teamwork Makes the Dream Work

As a mixed martial arts fan, I have researched how these guys train, watched documentaries of what it takes to get to the top level of the sport, and been to live events. I enjoy watching the talent that these athletes display. I am obviously a big fan, but more than that I have a ridiculous amount of respect for the fighters themselves. The one thing I have noticed is that the staff of coaches, sparring partners, doctors, and nutritionists that surround these guys are world class. They have boxing coaches, wrestling coaches, kickboxing coaches, ju-jitsu and grappling coaches, strength and conditioning coaches, and the list goes on and on. Some of these fighters will travel to different states and countries just to have the opportunity to train with the best coaches and learn from the best camps.

The fighters that have the natural talent, raw toughness, and best training and team, are the fighters that become champions and realize the dream of being the very best in the world. What they do not do is put some guy on their team who sits on the couch eating potato chips all day for a living. They do not put some guy on their team who sits around in his underwear blogging about how they could have won their last fight. The people on their team are people they trust, people that believe in them.

As a Christian, we have to take the same strategy. We have to be willing to grow and learn. We must build our dream team of coaches. As I mentioned earlier, the team I have in my life consists of my spouse, pastors, sponsor, and friends who hold me accountable. Not just anybody can make it on the team. These are people who believe in me, trust I am growing in my faith, and believe in the calling on my life. Sure there will be critics, but they will not be on my team! We must guard the streams of influence on our life and surround ourselves with the right people.

Protect the Environment of Restoration

MATTHEW 9:23-24 NIV

When Jesus entered the synagogue leader's house and saw the noisy crowd and people playing pipes, he said, "Go away. The girl is not dead but asleep." But they laughed at him.

There is an important element of restoration that we must note. It is the environment and atmosphere that we have around us. When Jesus went into this man's house, he went in with a mission in mind: to bring this little girl to back to life. When the scripture says, he "saw the noisy crowd and people playing pipes," it is referring to people weeping and playing songs of mourning. They were in the process of a funeral procession. But then Jesus shows up and ruins the funeral by bringing this little girl back to life!

If he did it in this story, then he can do it in your story! He can and will ruin the funeral for your destiny if you let Him! It just takes an element of faith and us being willing to choose what type of environment in which our restoration will take place. We must choose to protect it. We must guard it and even change it in order to see progress happen. It is the difference between a thermostat and a thermometer. A thermometer tells the temperature of a room, whereas a thermostat changes the temperature. Go ahead and change the atmosphere.

For me, it meant I had to hide some people from my Facebook stream and make some lists on Twitter of positive people that are encouraging. I had to resolve not to allow haters and negative people to just post comments and make whatever remarks they felt like. When they did, like Jesus in this passage, I cleared the room! We cannot be weak on this – we must confront the negative atmosphere and change it or it will choke out the life-giving restoration that God wants to do in our life. Some of us have lived in such an atmosphere of negativity our whole lives that we need to clear the room and drive out those negative influences!

Jesus walks into the room with a spirit of faith and changes the reality of what was happening. He doesn't even say that girl is dead but instead he says "asleep." It is kind of like he was saying that all these people had it twisted and they had no clue of what was really going on! He did not agree with them. He spoke what he believed to be true. Then they laughed at him. It is amazing to me that the Son of God was laughed at! Please see this – if He is going to get laughed at then so will we. It does not matter though, we must have more faith in God that we will succeed than the negative people have that we are going to fail.

Jesus Will Help You Get Up

> MATTHEW 9:25 NIV
>
> *After the crowd had been put outside, he went in and took the girl by the hand, and she got up.*

Jesus clears the room. He redeems the environment. Then the best part happens. He grabs the girl by the hand and *she got up*.

This is the message of this book. Jesus wants to grab you by the hand and help you get up. When he does grab your hand, you will get up. He will walk with you through the death of a dream or a relationship so you can see it was just "asleep" and He can wake it up! He will walk with you through whatever goes on in your life. Ultimately, He wants to walk with you through the process of restoration and help you reach your destiny.

It is our choice to do it. The heart of God is that His redemptive plan is executed in the world, but it starts with us and it starts in our hearts. My prayer for you is to experience complete and total restoration. I believe in you and believe you are created for greatness.

It is your time to get up.

www.ingramcontent.com/pod-product-compliance
Lightning Source LLC
Chambersburg PA
CBHW070852050426
42453CB00012B/2153